The Living Socrates

Introduction by George N. Shuster

President Emeritus, Hunter College

Drawings by Joseph Sheppard

Pearl Cleveland Wilson

The
Living
Socrates

The Man
Who Dared
to Question,
as Plato Knew Him

Stemmer House

Publishers, Inc. / *Owings Mills, Maryland* / 1975

A Barbara Holdridge Book

Printed and bound in the United States of America
First Edition

Library of Congress Cataloging in Publication Data

Wilson, Pearl Cleveland, 1882-
    The living Socrates.

    "A Barbara Holdridge book."
    Bibliography: p.
    1. Socrates.   I. Plato.   Dialogues.   English.
Selections.   II. Title.
B316.W524   183'.2 [B]   75-25021
ISBN 0-916144-00-3

To the memory of
EDWARD DELAVAN PERRY
for many years
Jay Professor of Greek
in Columbia University

Contents

Chapters

Drawings may be found on pages 4, 14-15, 26, 35, 46, 59, 62-63, 76, 82, 98-99, 108 and 117

Introduction

This is a book about a very great man written by a learned and distinguished woman who taught Greek literature for forty years. Socrates wrote nothing. What we know about him apart from a rather gossipy memoir by Xenophon is to be found in the *Dialogues* of Plato. The *Dialogue* was essentially a presentation and discussion of a problem or experience which paraphrased what the discussants had said. Plato had been a playwright before deciding to make Philosophy his life work, and this apprenticeship may help to explain why he was so successful in making what essentially is a series of interviews with Socrates so enduringly interesting. To be sure there were no tape recordings in those days, and Plato may well have idealized Socrates upon occasion. It is rather odd that nobody has tried earlier to do what Pearl Wilson has now accomplished—namely, to piece together what was said by the man who meant so much to Plato. Here is not just a beguiling essay but a wonderful collection of the texts in an excellent translation well suited to American readers. It is not a contribution to the enormous amount of scholarly writing about Greek philosophy but a superb addition to the literature which tries to teach. Today we believe that it is unnecessary and indeed impossible to study everything in high school or college. With the proper guidance people can teach themselves. I can only hope and wish that with the help of this book many will be able to do just this about one of the noblest and most inspiring men who ever lived.

Socrates, who died in 399 B.C., had been a soldier and a very good one, was married to Xanthippe who bore him three children, and spent a great deal of time in the streets of Athens arguing with anybody who wished to engage in a battle of wits. Pearl Wilson is quite skeptical of the notion that Xanthippe was a shrew and suggests that in a society which relied on slave labor, and pretty much relegated women to the nursery and the kitchen, she may just have been a little wittier and more sprightly than most of her sisters.

We speak of Socrates' habit of asking questions as his "method." This is a significant word. I take it to mean that as expounded in Plato's *Dialogues* it exemplified a way of examining great changes which had taken place in Greek education. Older Greek Society had been taught largely by memorizing passages from Homer and other poets and went to see and listen to the great plays of Aeschylus and Sophocles. But the Athenian education which Socrates now encountered was dealing with quite new and revolutionary concepts which could be summed up under the term Philosophy. On the one hand this asked questions about Nature and thus began the long road down which the Natural Sciences would later travel. With this Socrates concerned himself hardly at all. On the other hand it fostered moral skepticism as expounded by rhetoricians called sophists. The Athenians had fallen on evil times. Theirs had always been a rather democratically minded society as compared with their principal neighbors, Persia and Sparta. Military defeat intensified resistance to authority and above all weakened faith in the gods. Yet at the same time mystical cults flourished too, which in so far as Socrates is concerned were identified with the Oracle of Delphi. But in the background were the great mystical insights of the Persians filtering through what are called the views of the Orphic cults. We will never know very much about the impact of these mystical insights and reflections on the thinking of Socrates, except to be sure that they were present.

And so it may well be better to think of him in terms of moral and religious education. He was a sort of itinerant professor, not very tall or lean of figure and whose greying hair was not well combed or oiled. He walked about obviously deep in thought and not staring at anything in particular. But he attracted able young men and accepted hospitality so that he might talk with groups or what we may term "classes." One may doubt that Plato recorded them all. But it seems questionable that many modern professors conduct more seminars than he did. He accepted no monetary payment, and in this respect differed completely from the sophists who were professional rhetoricians, that is, teachers of the arts of persuading and influencing people. Some were able men and Socrates respected them. But the nibblers at authority whom the sophists fostered became the most popular sophist teachers, who invented quizzes which beguiled the Athenians.

One of the more familiar of these was the question: "Have you taken off your horns?" The teacher said that answering "Yes" was as ridiculous as answering "No." For an affirmative reply would mean that you had once had horns, while "No" would mean that you still had them. But of course one who taught in the spirit of Socrates would retort that the negative answer simply meant that you had never had them. The sophistic question was only a clever fraud. Such frauds were innumerable and very popular in a society which had neither TV nor competing newspapers.

I am sometimes reminded, as I reflect on these aspects of the Greek experience, of John Dewey. It seems to me that he must be called the most illustrious of American sophists. He certainly was an honorable and learned man; and after I came to know him I admired him very much. His reaction to Communism after he had visited Russia was very negative, and he had much to do with organizing American intellectual resistance to it. But he taught at a time when it seemed that the older schemata would no longer adequately serve the American educational purpose. The Bible had been subjected to so much textual criticism that its authority was seriously undermined, especially in the Torah schools from which so many excellent university students would graduate. Then there were the McGuffey Readers, which offered to public school children moral maxims and tales, reminding one interested in such matters, of Greek young people and the Homeric poems. But the new American generation of educators was pragmatic and concerned with community-building and opposition to unbridled capitalism. It was not literary in its basic orientation.

Dewey proposed his own solution of the underlying intellectual and educational problems, but even the Greek sophists, who wandered off in all directions themselves, might well have considered it vague. American teachers trained in the Dewey tradition began to attribute to their master aphorisms and conclusions which all but denied the sanity of the educational process. Thus there was a Middle Western professor who, when asked why girls could not spell or read efficiently, replied that it was far more important for them to learn how to bake a good cherry pie. This was Dewey's utilitarianism gone virtually mad. During the observance of the Dewey centennial, in which I participated, the principal Dewey scholars spent their time repudiating what lesser people had attributed to the master. I comment on these American experiences because they may help us to understand what Socrates was up against. No one could question the significance of some of the sophists. Nobody could deny that Protagoras was an able thinker, or that Euripides was a memorable playwright, although in so far as the Deities were concerned he professed the same negative outlook as Thomas Hardy would much later on. Of course in Greece Plato and Aristotle would go to battle with the sophists. In the United States there were critics too—Robert Hutchins, Mortimer Adler and, the greatest of them, William Ernest Hocking. All this may be ancient history but it may well return to haunt us.

It was of course Plato who amplified and deepened the thinking of Socrates. This he did in the first instance by setting forth his views of the relationships among education, philosophy and religion. Indeed, though he himself was a poet, he attacked the poetic educational tradition very sharply, seemingly because he was persuaded that the older Greek way of teaching would have to be abandoned, for the reason that it was beginning to do more harm than good. Philosophy had come to stay. His views are set forth most clearly in a treatise called the *Laws,* but the relationship between it and Socrates is already tenuous. Paul Elmer More, initially Princeton's first distinguished Sanskrit scholar, published his *Religion of Plato* in 1921. He dealt primarily with the continuing confrontation between the Greek philosopher's religious philosophy and that which in then recent times had drawn its inspiration from Kant and Hegel. It is still, I believe, a very good book, and though its first aim is not to discuss Socrates one can still see clearly how great the influence of that illustrious teacher was. For without a constant search for Justice and an awareness of the authority of the God, human society could not in Plato's opinion survive or thrive. Today the influence of Kant and Hegel, once so very great and perhaps not so pernicious as More thought, has been supplanted by that of Freud and Marx. They did profoundly alter human thought and human society. But today Freud's projections of pre-natal sexual experiences are so largely discredited that they are practically without influence, and Marx remains one of the greatest revolutionists in history but a very poor social scientist and economist, whose teachings have doomed a great part of the human race to virtual slavery. Perhaps—who knows?—mankind is now ready for a revival of Platonic thinking.

Plato's chief educational purpose, apart from his interest in mathematics and ideas, was the reform of Athenian society. But in this he did not succeed. How fortunate we inheritors of the English concepts of the Common Law and of Constitutionalism have been! For despite all our civil wars, both in Britain and the United States, we have nevertheless preserved our basic institutions and have supported them with such inspiring documents as Lincoln's *Gettysburg Address* and *Second Inaugural*. Never in its post-Platonic history has Greece been so fortunate.

Still I suppose that nobody can now live in a society like ours without upon occasion at least being appalled. To men and women of my age it must inevitably seem that a shadow fell over the earth in 1914, when the peoples of Europe marched off so blithely to war. From this they have never really returned, and in some ways—the nuclear armament ways in particular—the shadow is deeper and darker than it was then. It is true that the human race has owed its evolution to its continuing mastery of technology. How could it have survived at first without its ever improving mastery of fire, of cutting tools, and its discovery of medicinal herbs! Armed with its unique intelligence it arrived at a moment when other animals had no defense; indeed, became dependent. I can think of no more pathetic symbol of this than deer coming to a human door in winter hoping for food. But now technology has advanced to a point at which not only can man destroy all other animals but he can destroy himself.

How inadequately we can deal with the despoilers of our society! And not only in Czechoslovakia or Vietnam. In modern Turkey, capital punishment, as instituted by Ataturk, wiped out any number of crimes and offenses. There is no robbery in Istanbul, no begging as in Cairo. Yet who among us would wish to live in Turkey? In the United States a young man could shoot down the most illustrious of the surviving Kennedys without drawing more than a prison sentence subject to early parole. We are afraid to walk down our streets at night, anxious every time a woman drives her car after dark. I recollect from the last of my years in New York crimes of rape and murder so odious that I should not wish to talk about them. The leaders of our society cannot ban the guns which can kill them instantly. And our women, in spite of pills, diaphragms and other devices, can have the unwanted children in their wombs killed off as easily as they can have a diseased appendix removed. And yet very good preparatory schools and colleges teach young people that what Irving Babbitt once called a *frein vital,* a vital restraint based on the recognition of a moral order, is just simply out of date. This may be all right. But it also may not be.

I have so far refrained from suggesting that readers of this book concern themselves with abstruse problems of analysis such as they would encounter if they were graduate students of Philosophy in a modern university. Perhaps it is just as well if they are not. For the tendency almost always is, in so far as readers are concerned, to feel that any "single statement" can be philosophically or religiously convincing. But the "single statement" can only be true for those who read and approve any one such statement. Otherwise, even the least well informed of us can see that the statement was not really designed for him. It cannot take into account his special needs, his particular outlook.

And so the concept of "Platonic irony" has special significance for all of us, and of course it means Socratic irony as well. What can this signify other than that while we argue, we feel that we do not know *that much* about the subject? We cannot help realizing that while we may have acquired a great deal of knowledge about a problem or situation, somebody else may have come up with a fact or two which we did not discover for ourselves. Thus the earth turns around the sun, and the sun has spots. It is useless to doubt such facts. But we do not know why we are on a planet spinning around the sun or how long its rays will last. It is futile to suppose that we could be certain about any such thing. Therefore while we argue about something, even something very important in the life of the human race, it is necessary to realize that we can only be as certain of the full meaning of life as "the gods" permit us to be.

Perhaps the *Dialogue* which makes us see this most clearly in so far as Socrates and Plato are concerned is the *Symposium.* This is concerned with *Eros,* a term for the complex Socratic, Platonic character of Love. It can of course be read as an account of Socrates' unwillingness to take advantage of one of his students. This would be a grave simplification. The *Dialogue* is about two very serious philosophic concepts. First, there is the

question as to whether reason, here more clearly defined as common sense, can be sufficient to guide man along his journey to
truth and righteousness, but must be spurred on by a certain
madness, intoxication, symbolized by the drinking of wine. I am
simplifying things very much, but not too much, I hope, to assist
Miss Wilson's purpose. Let me recall from my early teaching days
that the stimulation of talking about a text to a group of students
would suddenly reveal to me a meaning other than the one I had
seen when I prepared the lecture. Socrates is essentially telling us
the same kind of thing. One must wait for the guidance of the
Eros, the love of truth, the imagination, the intoxication, if you
will, which is akin to the making of poetry. Therewith poetry
enters once more into the Socratic and Platonic scheme of things,
and indeed into their insight into the nature of the world.

And so we come to the tragic *Dialogues*, those which have to
do with the trial, conviction and death of Socrates. He was condemned by an ultra-conservative group which had come to power
in Athenian society, not for opposing the sophists but for being
one! These are great and very moving reports. They can mean
less to anyone who does not believe that the spirit of man has
everlasting life. But they can challenge even the most skeptical
and self-centered of us. As I have grown older I have thought
more and more about the differences and similarities between
Socrates and Jesus, upon whose lives and examples so many men
and women have patterned their actions and concerns. I am
thinking of course of the clean of heart and not of the fanatics.
Let us discuss the differences first.

Jesus died a Galilean only thirty years old, convinced that he
was God's son and would rise three days after his death. His
teaching, so imperfectly recorded for us in the Gospels, despite
their simplicity and beauty, was formed in the spirit of the great
Jewish prophets and probably also in that of some of the ascetic
communities which flourished in the neighboring desert. We
know at any rate about John the Baptist, whom Jesus considered
his great precursor and who preached in the desert and lived on
locusts and honey. (Salome, daughter of the mistress of Herod
the Roman, was induced by her mother to serve John's head on
a platter, thus exemplifying what many other mistresses would
desire to do throughout subsequent history.)

Jesus was also a great master of healing which only the Jewish tradition could have made manifest. For this was a free and holy people and it knew much about the spirit's command over the body. The year of Jesus' teaching in Galilee is, I think, unquestionably the most beautiful and remarkable year in human history. His mother was a Jewish girl. His story is a Jewish story. I am persuaded that Jesus went to Jerusalem to try to prevent an unsuccessful uprising against Rome and that he fell a victim to an anti-pacificist mob. This of course we will probably never know for sure.

Socrates also fell a victim to an ultra-conservative government. For other similarities I think we must go back again and again to the account of Jesus' final Seder (the "Last Supper") with his disciples and to Socrates' last discussions with his friends and disciples. These are the most beautiful documents in our literature. About oneself one has only to ask whether one would have wished to be there. Neither of them had to die. Socrates could have walked out of his prison. Jesus could easily have escaped from the mob. They believed that God, or in Socrates' case the God, would welcome them for testimony well given. This is what some of the noblest of Christians and Jews said to Hitler later on, or what great American leaders have proclaimed for the oppressed. And so how poorer off spiritually and ethically we would be if we did not have the final testimony of Socrates, as we have the final testimony of Jesus. Paul was Jesus' Plato. But his letters, beautiful and meaningful though they are, are not Dialogues. These *Dialogues* have magical beauty and are read by almost as many people as read the Bible.

I shall conclude by saying a little about Pearl Wilson and about why I have written this introduction. She lived and taught for many years simply, unselfishly and humbly. During more than twenty years I was the President of Hunter College in New York, which then enrolled many, many young women selected for their academic ability. The classical languages were taught well. So was much else. When I came to Hunter I was much impressed by the large number of excellent women scholars who taught there because of prejudices against employing them in the universities. They made Hunter a great seat of learning in many fields. But when I discovered that the College ranked fourth in the United States in terms of contributions to humanistic scholarship I was quite naturally impressed and even amazed. The classical languages and literature were taught especially well, as I could in some measure judge because I had majored in them and arrived at the blissful point where I could read Plato in Greek with little help from the dictionary. My doctoral dissertation was based on the classics too, though it was written in the then new field of Comparative Literature. To be sure, excellent women scholars taught classical studies at other colleges too, and I had known especially Vida Scudder at Vassar and Eleanor Duckett at Smith. But I think Pearl Wilson at Hunter was the most successful of them. She was a little woman but she never shied away from participation in college activities.

Classical studies continued to flourish at Hunter, while they were dying out elsewhere. One reason was the fact that we had a small group of girls from Greek families, who were interested in their tradition. I once listened to Henri Gregoire, then an eminent refugee scholar from a European university because of Hitler, tell a group of such students that theirs was the "language of the Holy Ghost." There was a professor at Hunter who taught in that manner but it was not Pearl Wilson's manner.

When, after obtaining her doctorate at Columbia University under the direction of a very competent scholar, she began to teach, the time was one in which the great translations, notably Jowett's in English, had been completed, and the critical histories of Greek philosophy had been written. Meanwhile the students of language, the Philologists, had been hard at work too and the texts available to students were almost unbelievably better than they had been. Indeed the German poet Goethe thought in his time that the texts and the translations based on them were so good that it would thenceforth not be necessary to read Greek in the original. Neither Pearl Wilson nor I quite believed that this was true, although I am sure, at least, that it has for some time been unnecessary to require a student to fight his way through the difficult texts of Aeschylus. But Pearl Wilson knew all this very well, and taught students to read and to love the original Greek, in all its subtleties. Among her students and friends were two girls, one of whom also attended a seminar which I taught in Renaissance poetry. The two girls founded Caedmon Records and were brilliantly successful. One is now the publisher of this book.

Meanwhile new reasons for reading Plato have appeared, and

I am persuaded that scholarship has never been more brilliant than it is now, particularly in the United States. I am no authority in such matters, but it would seem that the distinguished German nuclear physicist Heisenberg was the first to point out that Plato's thinking had most clearly anticipated the discoveries and theories of Einstein and the Quantum Physicists. At any rate we now have a number of learned books about Plato's Logic, for example. The range of the reflection of the great Greek philosopher may even yet not have been fully discovered. But Pearl Wilson has been concerned with what I believe is far more important. The "tragic *Dialogues*," which comment so profoundly on the nature and destiny of man, are read by more people in the United States than any other book except the Bible. How good it is that a great teacher has given the people a chance to read what is the *essence* of many of the *Dialogues!*

I am persuaded that humanistic teaching, provided either through the classroom or through reading, can save the culture of the United States from succumbing to its worst instincts. No one can make us return to our Puritan past. We are now prevailingly an urban society, and those who cater to such a society know only too well what human instincts are. But there does live on in all of us a deep desire for nobility of purpose and dignity. And many would rather be like Socrates than like the characters hunted down by the police. This multitude Pearl Wilson has all her life long kept very much in mind.

GEORGE N. SHUSTER
University of Notre Dame

September 1975

Preface

The name of Socrates is familiar to practically everyone. But a large proportion of the reading public has missed the experience of forming individual opinions of a surprising, and in some ways puzzling, man.

What made him unforgettable? Chiefly the writings of his understanding friend, Plato. But these are in ancient Greek, a barrier to most modern readers. Even when translated, his works fill too many pages—an absolutely forbidding obstacle.

Yet contained in Plato's *Dialogues,* though widely scattered, is an arresting portrayal of a unique character, deeply troubled by some things that trouble us today. All who knew him well were devoted friends. Partly because of this popularity, others hated or feared him.

This book is an attempt to present clearly for the perceptive reader the personality and thought of Socrates as shown in some of Plato's most dramatic *Dialogues,* with lively and fairly long quotations from them. Plato was not content to transmit only the philosophy of Socrates. He wanted to provide, for any born too late to meet the man himself, a way to approximate that experience.

P.C.W.

August 1975

"I shall seek always to know the truth
and to live in accord with it,
and I urge all others —
to the utmost extent of my power —
to join me in this effort."

1/ In a deteriorating city

Ancient Athens, during the life of Socrates, was losing the almost incredible glory that had made the poet Pindar call her "brilliant and honored upholder of Hellas, miraculous city." That was his tribute to her for saving Greece from conquest by the Persian king, Darius. Her victories on land at Marathon in 490 B.C., and on the sea at Salamis ten years later, were important in ending the Persian despots' attempts to add part of Europe to their vast empire.

In the next fifty years Athens remained at her highest peak. She was recognized as the most important city in the Greek-speaking world, which included not only the peninsula, but southern Italy and Sicily, as well as some cities of western Asia and northeastern Africa near the Mediterranean Sea. During those years she developed a civilization where freedom under law invigorated an entire people, so that they embodied in literature, in art and in political life ideals that can still inspire those who study them.

Socrates was born in 469 B.C., somewhat before the middle of that fortunate period. When he came of age at eighteen, the great sculptor Phidias was making noble statues, Polygnotus was painting frescoes in temples and public buildings, the building of the Parthenon had begun. All of the impressive tragedies of Aeschylus had been performed, as well as a few by Sophocles and one by Euripides. The fame of Athens had spread through the Greek world, and men of achievement in various fields came to spend time there and display their talents. Wherever one turned, there was an upsurge of creative ability.

Socrates was thirty-eight in 431 B.C., at the beginning of the disastrous Peloponnesian war, which was to continue, off and on, for thirty years. In the second year of the war, a great plague fell upon Athens and lasted about two years. The horrors of war and plague together destroyed much that had been fine in Athenian life and character. Great men lived afterward and left works of inestimable value, but life in Athens was never again what it had been in her lamentably short period of glory.

Even before the war started, Socrates had noticed a tendency among Athenians to lower their standards in a way he thought dangerous. This had begun earlier with their interest in a new study taught by men called sophists, which in some ways had been at first a help, but which later developed a preoccupation with superficial effects whose glitter often obscured actual truth.

The study was originated by Corax at Syracuse in Sicily. He called it rhetoric, and took as pupils men who wanted to learn how to use their language better in speaking and writing. When the reputation of Corax was at its height, his first pupil, Tisias, brought the study to Athens, where it was received with great enthusiasm.

Socrates spent much of his life in trying to induce his fellow Athenians to test their statements by clear reasoning and ever finer discrimination, in order to avoid the mental confusion this "rhetoric" might produce.

Plato, in his *Dialogues*, has given us, with fascinating variety, some understanding of how Socrates did this. Those chosen for presentation here are only a small number of them, perhaps the most dramatic.

In the later part of the fifth century B.C., most Athenians knew Socrates, at least by sight. Among athletic, straight-nosed men, he was conspicuous for his portly body and his wide, turned-up nose, both of which made him look as if he had walked out of a comic performance, forgetting to discard his make-up. One of the three contemporaries who wrote about him was the great comic poet Aristophanes, whose plays, presented frequently throughout the Peloponnesian war, always called for peace.

Comedies at this time usually presented exaggerated carica-tures of well-known people and recent incidents. They were closer in spirit to political cartoons in our newspapers than to anything now written for the stage. In *The Clouds*, which Aristophanes himself considered his best play, Socrates is shown presiding over a philosophical school. When, at sight of an actor looking exactly like the man they saw daily on the street, the first audience burst into prolonged laughter, Socrates himself rose from his seat in the theater so that everyone could enjoy the perfect resemblance. Another laugh followed when the actor proclaimed solemnly, "I tread the air and contemplate the sun." The word "contemplate" in Greek also means "look down upon." The pun was intentional.

Yet, ridiculously untrue as much of this comedy is, there are moments which show Socrates as his earlier friends knew him.

When *The Clouds* was produced at a festival in 423 B.C., Socrates was about forty-six and Aristophanes twenty-three. Plato and Xenophon, the other two contemporaries who wrote about Socrates, were not in the theater, neither having reached the age of ten. Unlike the playwright, both wrote about Socrates after his death in 399 B.C., Plato beginning very soon, Xenophon fifteen or more years later.

Xenophon admired Socrates, but not profoundly enough to follow his advice. This he tells quite frankly at the beginning of the third book of his *Anabasis*. A Greek friend who had become a general in the army of Cyrus, the Persian prince, wrote a letter urging Xenophon to join him. When showing this tempting letter to Socrates, Xenophon was surprised by the older man's remark that to go might endanger Xenophon's standing in Athens, for Cyrus had aided her enemy, Sparta. Socrates, observing his young friend's still undiminished eagerness, then suggested that he should consult the oracle at Delphi, which was a center of international information.

On the way to Delphi, Xenophon's desire evidently took complete possession of him. What he asked was, "To which divinities should I sacrifice and pray in order to be safe on the journey I am about to take and return alive?"

Socrates reproached him for this, but accepted his decision. Time proved that the older man had been right, for Xenophon, during his absence, was exiled from Athens for having aided an enemy. There is no indication that he ever returned to his native city.

Back in Greece and forbidden to return to Athens, Xenophon wrote his *Anabasis*, recounting the Persian expedition and his famed march to the sea, leading ten thousand Greek soldiers.

He wrote also about Socrates, whose trial had been held two years after Xenophon had gone to Persia. The beginning of his *Memorabilia* is an emphatic defense of the man he admired, as testimony that the jury's decision twenty years earlier had been unjust. Then follow accounts of what Socrates said on different occasions. Surprise has sometimes been expressed that there is no talk of philosophy, but only of subjects of a practical nature. But the outlook and achievements of Xenophon were exactly of that nature, and there are many passages in Plato's *Dialogues* indicating that it was the habit of Socrates to meet men on their own ground, discussing whatever they were likely to have thought enough about to form an opinion.

It was another admiring young friend, Chairephon, who had—without intention—caused Socrates to adopt what was to become the guiding purpose of his life. The enthusiastic devotion of this young man often carried him beyond all bounds, earning him the ridicule of Aristophanes in three comedies. When he felt that the provocative talk of Socrates was not receiving the attention it deserved, Chairephon astonished Athens by going to consult the oracle at Delphi.

"Is anyone wiser than Socrates?" he asked.

Receiving the answer that there was no one wiser, he came back to tell everybody he met.

Yet, to his surprise, Socrates was not pleased. He had studied the works of early Greek philosophers, but had not been convinced by their explanations. The one thing of which he remained certain was his own ignorance. He could not accept the answer of the oracle, but resolutely set out to prove it false.

Athenians had recently finished developing their democratic government and many were active politicians. Socrates had intentionally kept out of political life, but certain that they knew much of which he was ignorant, he wanted to talk to them now. There was no difficulty about this, for Athenians spent most of their time in public places. Socrates began to discuss with one after another not only politics, but other important subjects.

To his amazement, he found that he could not call even the most expert politicians truly wise. They were ignorant of much outside their own field. What most troubled Socrates was that, because of their political eminence, they were ready to make positive statements about many things of which they knew absolutely nothing. This Socrates was careful never to do, and he decided.

"In that way, I suppose I might be called wiser.

"But I will talk to the poets. They must be far wiser than I who never composed a single line of verse."

Discovering that not even one was able to explain what he had written, Socrates concluded that poets were guided by inspiration, not reasoning. Yet they were often quoted as authorities.

He had the same experience among fine craftsmen. They were equally ready to praise or condemn something to which they had not given a moment of discriminating thought, but were merely repeating what they had heard somewhere—for Athenians were incessant talkers!

Finally Socrates felt he must admit that the statement Chairephon brought back from the oracle was true, but in a sense different from what everyone had inferred. Socrates was wiser than others because he was fully aware of his own ignorance.

Too many Athenians, he observed, were fascinated by striking phrases that sounded clever, but conveyed no real truth. If this habit continued, it would before long blunt any finer perceptions they might possess. Only true knowledge would correct it, but that could not be gained easily or quickly, for it must stand the test of thorough reasoning. Socrates resolved to devote the rest of his life to making people realize this. In a rapidly deteriorating society, where citizens too clearly displayed the arrogant ignorance Socrates probed, the result was to prove fatal.

We may be certain that neither *The Clouds* of Aristophanes nor Xenophon's *Memorabilia* would have caused the name of Socrates to appear as often as it does today, more than two thousand years later. It catches the eye even in newspapers of our western land, not yet discovered by Europeans when Socrates was alive.

Why did this come about? Chiefly, it was because of the deep impression Socrates made on a young man, named Aristocles by his father, but nicknamed "Widefellow," since he had particularly broad shoulders, and classified ever since by librarians under that name, Plato.

A noted philosopher in his own time, he had other abilities as well, one being a gift of characterization. In a few words he could convey to a reader anyone's outstanding traits, often with ironic effect. He wrote the beautiful ancient Greek with sensitivity, and when he wished, with astonishing power. Judged by a literary standard, his finest achievement was the series of word portraits he drew of Socrates in different situations.

Everybody in Athens knew that wherever Socrates came, people gathered round him, especially young men. While Plato was a child, his two much older brothers gleefully talked about hearing Socrates, by brilliant reasoning, reduce a pompous boaster to utter confusion. The boy ardently wished that he could have been there with them. As soon as he attained manhood, he made it his habit to join any group that was listening to Socrates. For ten years this was an important part of the young man's life.

Then, when Plato was about thirty, the man who had opened so many vistas to him was sentenced to death "for corrupting the young men of Athens."

Shock left Plato desolate. Gone was the intellectual stimulus and spiritual inspiration that had made life worth while. Gone, when Athens needed it most.

But Plato could never forget. Remembered also were conversations of which others had told him. If he could write all of these, if he could make Socrates alive again as he himself would always feel him, then the world would not after all be without the gifts of that far-seeing teacher who claimed that he was *not* teaching, but only trying, with others, to learn.

Soon after the death of Socrates, Plato began to write the *Dialogues* in which Socrates is the chief character, and from which the material in this book is drawn.

In the latest years of his life, Plato wrote what is known as the *Laws*. It is his longest work, also written in dialogue form, but without Socrates. The dominant figure is simply "an Athenian," but many identify him with Plato himself. In the *Laws*, one may find conclusions relating to ethics, education and lawmaking, reached by Plato after a lifetime of thought. Through his writings, the young man who had sat modestly at Socrates' feet became himself one of the most renowned philosophers of the ages.

Because Plato observed, understood and in the *Dialogues* portrayed so vividly how Socrates went about the work he had undertaken, a thoughtful reader today may suddenly be surprised to find Socrates teaching him as well, and he may even find himself struggling, as so many others did, to evade the keen edge of that master's perspicacity.

2 / A day at the wrestling school, and a charm for the young

In the groups that gathered about Socrates there were only men and boys. Athenians, in this century, kept their wives and daughters strictly sheltered in the home. A belief of Socrates not shared by most of his Athenian friends was that women differed from men only in physical strength, and in the kind of training to which they were restricted in Athens. Plato shows Socrates quoting with approval the words of two women—Diotima of Mantinea and Aspasia, who had come from Miletus.

Handsome young men in fifth-century Athens received admiration and attention resembling that given to beautiful women in the age of chivalry. Conspicuous among them was Charmides, whose name is given to one of the *Dialogues*.

After returning late one night from a military campaign, Socrates rose in the early morning, happy to be home again in sunny Athens. He hurried to one of his favorite meeting places, the wrestling school opposite the government office. The moment he appeared in the doorway, both the young athletes and the men watching them turned excitedly towards him. Chairephon ran to be first to grasp his hand.

"Socrates!" he cried joyfully. "How did you get through the battle?"

"As you see," Socrates smiled.

"The only news we have is that many were killed."

"Unfortunately that is true."

"Who escaped?" countless voices asked. "Sit down and tell us."

After replying to all their questions, Socrates had one for them.

"How are things here?" he inquired. "Are you still interested in philosophy? Has any of your younger friends become outstanding for his knowledge while I was away?"

Several shouted at once, "Charmides!"

"My cousin," an older man named Critias exclaimed. "He was still a boy when you left. Now he has already begun to be a philosopher and something of a poet. Besides, we all agree that he is the handsomest lad in Athens." Glancing toward the door, he added, "There he comes now."

To Socrates, youth was always beautiful, but the young man he saw moving forward with athletic grace was indeed breathtakingly attractive. All stopped their activity to gaze at him, the youngest boys standing motionless in wonder, as if they were seeing that a statue made by the great Phidias had suddenly come alive. With Charmides were companions of his own age, laughing and making fun of one another.

"What do you think of him, Socrates?" Chairephon asked eagerly. "Hasn't he a beautiful face?"

"Surpassingly beautiful," Socrates responded, "if he has one other thing as well."

"What?" Critias asked sharply, a little indignant.

"A soul equally beautiful."

"That he certainly has," said Critias.

"Then why not call him, so he can reveal his soul to us?"

"Gladly." Critias turned to an attendant. "Go, boy," he said. "Tell Charmides I want to introduce him to a doctor who will cure the pain he was telling me about."

When the boy ran off, Critias said, "He has been complaining of headaches. Can't you pretend that you know a cure?"

Charmides came at once and sat down between the two men. His young friends gathered around, creating much laughter as each tried to get nearer to Charmides by pushing others away.

"Here is the man," Critias said, "who can cure your pain."

Looking at Socrates, Charmides asked respectfully if he knew a cure for headache.

"Yes," Socrates replied. "I learned it from a Thracian while I was serving in the army. It is a kind of leaf that must be accompanied by a certain charm. If the person repeats the charm while he uses the leaf, he will become well. But without the charm the leaf will not cure."

"Do tell me the charm," Charmides said eagerly, "so I may write it down."

"If you can persuade me to do so?" Socrates asked, and then added in a teasing manner, "or perhaps even if you don't?"

They both laughed, and Socrates knew that he had taken a step toward directing the lad's thought, for a shared laugh draws young and old together.

"If I can persuade you, of course, Socrates."

"Oh, you think you know my name. Are you quite sure?"

"Indeed I am. My friends have often talked about you, and I remember seeing you with Critias when I was a small boy."

"Good!" Socrates exclaimed. "Then you know about my way of talking—how I like to examine a subject thoroughly. Are you ready to listen to my explanation of this charm?"

"Indeed I am."

"This charm will do more than cure a headache. Perhaps you have heard one of our doctors say—if a patient, for instance, has trouble with his eyes—that the whole body must be treated. The part will be cured with the whole. Have you heard something like that?"

"Yes, I have."

"Would you be willing to agree?"

"I would."

"A Thracian doctor told me that their king, whom they reverence almost as if he were a god, maintained that Greek doctors were right about this, but they ought to go farther. One should not try to cure the body without first curing the soul, for all good and evil originate there, and a part can never be really well unless the whole is well. The soul can be cured by the right words, and the thought they make clear. The words are a charm to implant *sophrosyne* in the soul. Where that is, health is soon imparted to the whole body."

(The Greek word *sophrosyne*, consisting of four syllables, has no exact English equivalent. It implies knowledge, but also moderation, self-mastery and a sane and healthy attitude toward life.)

Socrates continued: "The Thracian compelled me to swear a solemn oath that I would not give anyone the leaf without the charm. If you will let me implant *sophrosyne* in your soul, I will give you the leaf."

Critias interrupted: "The headache will be an unexpected benefit to the lad, if the pain in his head leads him to improve his mind. I can tell you, Socrates," he continued, "that Charmides is as remarkable for *sophrosyne* as he is for his good looks."

"If he has *sophrosyne* already," said Socrates, "I can give him the cure for his headache at once. But I want to be certain. Tell me, dear Charmides, have you the gift of *sophrosyne,* as your cousin says?"

"I cannot say either yes or no," Charmides replied. "If I say I do not possess it, I will be contradicting Critias, my guardian. But if I say I do, that will be praising myself. Either would be offensive."

With characteristic friendliness, Socrates said, "I understand your feeling. Let's examine the matter together, and begin by deciding what the word *sophrosyne* means. What is your opinion?"

After thinking about how, when he was younger, his elders kept telling him how he should behave, Charmides said, "I believe it means doing things in an orderly and quiet way. One might say it means quietness."

"Many people do consider that a quiet person has *sophrosyne,*" Socrates agreed, "but let us see whether they are right. Do you believe that *sophrosyne* is good?"

"I certainly do."

"But when you were learning to write, did you do better by learning to form the letters quietly or quickly?"

"Quickly."

He gave similar answers about learning how to wrestle and how to play the lyre.

"Then," said Socrates, "in all that concerns bodily actions, we agree that not quietness but quickness is better and shows a higher degree of self-mastery. How is it with learning? Is it better to learn quietly and slowly, or quickly? And is it better to understand anything said as quietly as possible, or as quickly as possible?"

They came to the conclusion that it was true of the mind as

well as of the body that in many types of activity quickness was better than quietness, so they were obliged to discard the definition of *sophrosyne* first given by Charmides.

"But we must not let ourselves be discouraged," said Socrates positively. "Perhaps we can find a better definition. Look within yourself and see if you can discover what effect *sophrosyne* has upon you. Don't be afraid, but tell me plainly."

The lad paused. He knew that he would be ashamed to do certain things—to praise himself, for instance, as he had remarked a short time before. So he said, "It keeps a modest person from

doing anything of which he would be ashamed, so perhaps *sophrosyne* is modesty."

Thinking for himself, Charmides had taken a step forward. Now he considered *sophrosyne* not as something externally imposed upon a person, but as an ethical principle within the person and controlling his action.

Socrates, however, soon showed that modesty was not a complete definition.

But he had already succeeded in interesting Charmides, who suddenly ventured, "O Socrates, I've just remembered hearing

someone say that *sophrosyne* was attending to one's own business. Do consider whether this is true."

"You young rascal!" exclaimed Socrates. "You got that from Critias—or maybe someone else."

"Not from me," said Critias. "I never told him that."

"What difference does it make who said it?" Charmides asked.

"None at all," said Socrates. "The important thing is whether it is true or not. It sounds like a riddle. The man who said it seems to have said one thing when he meant another."

After a few other questions, Socrates asked Charmides, "Do you think a state would be well organized if it had a law compelling every man to weave his own garments—and also wash them himself—and to make his own shoes?"

"No, I think it would not," Charmides answered.

"Yet if well organized, its laws would cultivate *sophrosyne* in its citizens?"

"Of course."

"Then doing one's own business and *sophrosyne* would not be identical?"

"Evidently not."

"That," said Socrates, "is why I claimed that the man who gave this definition must have had a hidden meaning. Otherwise he would have been utterly foolish. Was he a fool, Charmides?"

"By no means. I thought him a very wise man."

"Then what is the meaning of a man's doing his own business? Can you tell me?"

"I certainly don't know, Socrates. And perhaps the man who said it didn't know what he really meant." With a glance toward Critias, Charmides laughed a little.

Socrates was now certain that it had been Critias who made the statement originally. He had been restless from the moment it was first mentioned, appearing eager to take part in the argument, while Charmides plainly felt unable to support the definition. Critias now became angry, as a tragic poet might be angry with an actor who spoiled the effect of his verse.

"Do you imagine, Charmides," he burst out, "that the author of the definition did not understand the meaning of his own words just because you don't understand them?"

Socrates intervened to prevent irritation from developing further.

"My dear Critias," he said, "the lad is too young to be expected to understand. But you, who are so much older and have studied so long, may know what this definition really means. If you do, and if you agree with its author, I would rather consider with you whether it is true or false."

Critias was delighted; and Charmides, obviously relieved, followed their argument with keen attention.

In the end, after examining several definitions, they found none of them acceptable.

"In spite of all our striving," Socrates admitted, "we have been unable to discover what it really is that we call *sophrosyne*. For myself it does not matter very much, but for your sake, Charmides, I am profoundly distressed. For I believe that *sophrosyne* is a great good. If you really possess it, I consider you indeed blest. Examine yourself carefully to discover if you have it. For if that is so, you do not need the charm."

"I don't know whether I have it or not," Charmides declared with a laugh. "But what I do know, Socrates, is that I need to be charmed by you every day until you say I have learned enough."

3 / A genial
first course
in thinking

Socrates could interest even a young boy in logical reasoning. He fully understood the interests and viewpoint of the very young, as is evident in his first talk with Lysis. Seeing that this boy showed the result of good Athenian training at home and school, Socrates set out to make the child think for the first time about a principle behind the discipline he had readily accepted. It was an entirely new experience for Lysis, but he responded to the kind of skillful leading that is called the Socratic method. The conclusion reached was one toward which Socrates often struggled, in a different way, to bring mature Athenians.

Walking along the road outside the wall of Athens, Socrates came upon a group of young men, one of whom left the rest to hurry toward him.

"O Socrates," he shouted happily, "where are you going?"

"To the Lyceum, Hippothales," Socrates answered with a smile.

"Oh, no! You're not going there. No, indeed. You're coming right here to us," the lad asserted.

"What do you mean by 'here'?" Socrates demanded.

"Why, here!" the lad repeated, as he pointed to an enclosure with the door standing open. "This is where many of us spend our time now."

"What is the place? and what do you do there?"

"A wrestling school for younger boys that has just opened." He laughed, then admitted, "We come here chiefly to talk."

"He comes here hoping to meet Lysis," said Ctesippus. "He's quite mad about that boy. Why, he even reads poems to Lysis that he wrote himself, in praise of the boy's famous ancestors and the victories they won at the great games."

"That's not the way to win a boy's friendship," said Socrates. "You are more likely to bore him."

"He certainly bores us," Ctesippus declared.

"Then tell me," said Hippothales, "what I should talk about in order to interest him."

"That's not easy to say. But if you bring him to me, I will show you what I mean."

"I can manage that," said Hippothales. "Just go in here and sit down, and begin to talk with Ctesippus. Lysis will come over to you at once, for he is very fond of listening."

They went in together and saw that the boys were all in white because it was the day of a festival. The sacrifices had been completed, and the boys had immediately settled down in the courtyard to play with dice.

Hippothales led the way into a large dressing-room. In one corner a group was playing with all kinds of dice, which they took from little baskets. Others stood around them, watching the game.

Hippothales whispered to Socrates, "The one still wearing his garland is Lysis."

They went to a part of the room far enough away to be undisturbed, and began to talk. Lysis had seen them enter and knew that the man with them must be Socrates. No one else was just this short and stout, with a face like a comic mask, or would be surrounded by such an eager crowd of young men. Menexenus, a somewhat older friend of Lysis, had often spoken of him.

Socrates, who always noticed more than anyone realized, saw that Lysis kept turning from the players to look in his direction, as if wanting to join his group, but feeling too shy. When Me-

nexenus entered from the court, Lysis hurried to his side and they
came over together.

Understanding the boy's shyness, Socrates did not speak to him
directly. "Well, Menexenus," he said, "which of you two boys is
the older?"

"We argue about that," said Menexenus with a laugh. (This
would not surprise anyone familiar with the complicated Athenian calendar.)

"I suppose you also hold different opinions about which belongs to the nobler family?" Socrates continued.

"Yes, indeed."

"And about which is the more handsome?"

The boys burst out laughing at such a question. After the three
had laughed together, Lysis was no longer too shy to speak, but
answered along with Menexenus.

"You are friends, aren't you?" Socrates asked.

"Yes, we are," said both.

"So I can't ask which is richer, for I remember the old saying
that the possessions of friends belong to both alike."

They were interrupted by someone who came in from the court
to say the wrestling master wanted Menexenus outside.

Socrates had been about to ask which was wiser, so leading to
a serious discussion. Now, however, he began to keep his promise
to Hippothales by showing how one might interest his friend.

"I suppose, Lysis," he said, "that your father and mother love
you dearly?"

A curious thing to ask, Lysis thought, but he answered without
hesitation, "Yes, they do."

"Then they must want you to be as happy as possible?"

"Of course."

"Do you think anyone is really happy who is prevented from
doing what he likes?"

"No, I certainly don't."

"Then if your father and mother love you and want you to be
happy, they undoubtedly do all they can to bring this about."

"Of course."

"They let you do whatever you wish, never rebuking you or
preventing you from doing what you most desire."

This startled the boy. "Oh, but they do, Socrates," he said emphatically. "They keep me from doing a lot of things."

"Is it true that they want you to be happy, yet prevent you from doing what will make you so?"

Lysis was puzzled. This didn't sound reasonable, but he knew it often happened.

"Let's consider some examples," Socrates suggested. "For instance, if you suddenly wanted to drive one of your father's chariots in a race, holding the reins yourself—would they allow that?"

The thought was exciting, but the boy knew it couldn't happen.

"They wouldn't think of it for a moment," he said.

"Who would be allowed to drive?"

"The charioteer hired by my father."

"But perhaps they would let you drive the mule-team, even using the whip?"

"Let me whip the mules? Never!"

"Can't the mules be whipped?"

"Oh, yes. But only by the mule-driver."

"Is he a slave or a free man?"

"A slave."

"So your father lets a slave do what you would enjoy doing, but he will not let you, even though you are the son he loves?"

Again Lysis was puzzled and could say nothing.

"At least they allow you to control yourself, don't they?"

"Oh, no. Not always."

"Who does control you?"

"Our *paidagogos*, of course." (This word designated the slave who took the boy to and from school, telling him how to behave on the way.)

"So you, who will grow up to be a free citizen, are actually controlled by a slave?"

"Of course. He's ours." Apparently Lysis would not be expected to obey the slave of any other family.

"Once you get to school, do the teachers control you?"

"Oh, don't they just? In more ways than I could tell you!"

"Your father certainly puts a great many masters over you, though you are the free son of a free man. But how about your mother? She wants you to be happy, I'm sure. When you come home, she lets you do whatever you like with her spindle or her loom."

That made Lysis laugh. "She would slap me if I even touched them."

"Your parents certainly keep you from doing many things you might enjoy, and your father puts many masters over you, though a slave has only one master."

"Oh, that's simply because I'm not of age," Lysis said contentedly as if it explained everything.

"I rather think that's not the reason," Socrates said gently. "Let's consider a different situation. There are some things, I believe, that they let you do without making you wait till you are of age. For instance, when they want something read to them, don't they often ask you do to it?"

"Yes, they do."

"And when you want to play the lyre, they don't forbid you to touch it till you are of age. They let you tune it and strike the strings with your fingers or with the plectrum, whichever you wish, don't they?"

"Yes."

"Then why is it, Lysis, that they let you do these things, but not the others?"

"I suppose it's because I know how to do these things, but not the others."

"Exactly, my friend! You see it is not age, but knowledge that is important."

Lysis had reached this conclusion by his own mental effort, which delighted Socrates. Because he wanted this to make a lasting impression on the boy's mind, Socrates carried the idea to its extreme.

"Whenever," he said, "your father comes to believe you understand his affairs better than he does himself"—Lysis laughed at the absurdity as Socrates paused—"on that very day he will hand them over to you to manage, won't he?"

The boy laughed even more, but managed to say, "I suppose."

"And you may be sure that the man who lives next door will follow your father's example as soon as he holds the same belief. What about the whole Athenian people? When they believe you have enough knowledge, won't they all entrust their affairs to you?"

By this time Lysis was laughing so hard that he could barely articulate, "Yes."

It was all ridiculous, of course, and utterly impossible, but Socrates was rewarding the boy for his mental effort and amusing him by a picture of the entire population of the great city seeking the help of his knowledge. Never had Lysis been led to imagine anything so astounding.

At that moment Menexenus returned. As he came through the door, Lysis whispered quickly, "O Socrates, ask Menexenus the questions you have been asking me." The boy who had been too shy to come over to Socrates alone was now completely at ease with him.

"You can ask him yourself, Lysis, at some other time, for I know you concentrated on what we were saying."

"I certainly did."

"But be careful," Socrates said, "to recall it accurately, so that all you say will be perfectly clear. If you have forgotten anything, ask me about it the next time we meet."

"I'll do that, Socrates. But talk to him about something else now, so that I may listen."

"Very well, I will, since you wish it. But be ready to come to my assistance if Menexenus starts to contradict me. Don't you know that he always wants to argue?"

"Indeed I do. That's why I want you to talk with him."

"So that the laugh may be on me?"

"Oh no! So that you may refute him as he has often refuted me."

"That won't be easy. He is clever. And Ctesippus, who has taught him, is here listening."

"Never mind who is here, Socrates. Go ahead. Ask him something."

"Evidently I shall have to," said Socrates.

"What are you talking about over there?" Ctesippus suddenly called out. Don't keep it to yourselves. Let us share it."

"Well, I will," responded Socrates. "Lysis said he didn't understand a statement I made, but he thinks Menexenus will, and wants me to ask him."

"Good! Ask him right away."

"Pay close attention, Menexenus," Socrates began. "Even when I was a boy, I began to desire one thing more than anything else. Some boys look forward to the time when they may have a horse, or a dog, some hope to become rich, others to be elected to a high political office. About these things I have always been indifferent. I wanted to have a good friend—more than I wanted a quail or a cock, or even a horse and a dog. Now that I have seen you two boys, Menexenus and Lysis, I think you are each most fortunate to have gained, while you are still so young, a devoted friend. Yet I do not know what makes one person become the friend of another, so I want to learn this from you. Tell me, Menexenus, when one person is attracted to another, is it the one who is attracted who becomes the friend, or the one who attracts, or does it make no difference?"

"No difference at all," he said.

So began a long discussion. Various theories were considered, such as attraction based on similarity, or on unlikeness, also the attachment of a boy to someone older whom he wishes to resemble. Before they were able to reach a conclusion that would bear the test of close reasoning, they were interrupted by the *paidagogoi* of both Menexenus and Lysis, who insisted that it was time for the boys to be on their way home.

As they reluctantly obeyed, Socrates said, "Now, Lysis and Menexenus, the laugh is on me, old as I am, along with you. All who have been listening to us will go away saying that we three are friends, and I agree that we are. Yet we have not been able to find out what a friend really is."

4

The rivals:

"How to win friends and influence people"

In his effort to make the young men of Athens develop their power to reason and to think philosophically, Socrates was opposed by rivals who made a strong appeal to all who were tempted by the promise of quick success. Men called sophists rose to prominence in the Greek cities of Sicily and southern Italy early in the fifth century B.C. They were public lecturers and teachers, who charged high fees for the courses they offered. They claimed that these courses would prepare anyone to speak in a way that would influence all who heard. (One is irresistibly reminded of *How to Win Friends and Influence People.*)

The earliest of the sophists is said to have been Corax (a name identical with the Greek word for the bird *crow.*) He was a native of Syracuse in Sicily, who accepted pupils and wrote a handbook on the art of persuasion, which he called rhetoric. His popularity was at its height when Socrates was born. An amusing anecdote about him and his first pupil, Tisias, who later came to Athens, shows a danger inherent in this kind of teaching.

Corax, unlike later sophists, did not at first require that his fee be paid before starting the course. Tisias, after completing it, refused to pay, so Mr. Crow took the matter to court. There Tisias declared, "Before I started, Mr. Crow, you promised you would teach me to persuade anyone to do whatever I wanted. Let me now persuade you not to ask for your fee. If you still demand it, you did not do what you promised, therefore I owe you nothing."

It is noteworthy that no Athenian was a famous sophist. But many sophists visited Athens and received high fees there. Prodicus, from an island near Athens, was the first to distinguish the different shades of meaning to be found in synonyms. Protagoras, from a city in Thrace, became renowned for a statement often quoted: "Man is the measure of all things." By this he indicated

that it was no use to try to discover truth, for there was no such
thing. There were only opinions of different individuals. The best
thing for a man to learn was how to make others accept his
opinion. Gorgias, from Sicily, was more concerned with the impressive way something could be said than with whether it was
true, or even had much meaning. When he came to Athens at
the head of an embassy in 427 B.C., and addressed the Athenian
Assembly, the younger listeners were completely carried away by
the dazzling brilliancy of his speech. It sounded so marvelous
that they never asked themselves if any important thought lay
beneath the words.

Those three sophists were men of ability, and some of the
things they taught had value. But Thrasymachus, from a Greek
city in Asia Minor, was vain and inclined to bluster. Since he was
unable to argue logically, a skillful opponent like Socrates could
easily reduce him to a state of confusion, whereupon he became
angry and insulting. He believed there was no such thing as
moral obligation. What people called right was merely conven-
tion, imposed by a ruler or a community for the advantage of the
power that prescribed it.

Others went to absurd extremes. Among them were two conspicuous brothers, who spent much time in Athens, though they
were not citizens. Socrates had sufficient opportunity to observe
their method on a day when he had been watching athletes in

their school at the Lyceum. Rising to leave, he felt his "familiar sign," and accordingly sat down again. This sign, as his friends knew, had first come to him in childhood. It checked him suddenly, and for no apparent reason, when he was about to speak or to move. He had discovered that whenever he obeyed it, something occurred to make him glad he had done so. Consequently, obedience had soon become a habit.

On this occasion, the sophist brothers entered, accompanied by a number of admirers. They all walked up and down together, the sophists apparently showing off. But as soon as young Cleinias came in, and immediately went to sit with Socrates, the brothers whispered together, then moved over to join the two, bringing their followers. Cleinias belonged to a distinguished family. The possibility of acquiring him as a pupil was too good an opportunity for the brothers to miss.

Socrates greeted them and introduced the youth, saying, "These two men, Cleinias, possess wisdom in no small degree and in more than one field. They can teach a man how to become an excellent general; also how to defend himself in court."

The brothers laughed scornfully.

"That is only a side line of ours now," declared one.

"Then your chief work must be extraordinary," said Socrates. "Do tell us what it is."

"We make a man both excellent and successful. What's more, we do this in the best and quickest way, with no waste of time."

"By Zeus!" exclaimed Socrates, "this is something! Do pardon what I said about you just now. But tell me, both of you, if what you claim is really true. It is so sweeping an assertion that you can hardly wonder at my hesitating to accept it."

"It is absolutely true," said one.

"You may be sure of that," added the other.

"Then you two men have a greater power than the mighty ruler of the vast Persian empire. Will you show me this wisdom of yours?"

"That's exactly what we came here to do," said one, "to display our power and to teach, if anyone is willing to learn."

"We all are, I believe," declared Socrates with a gesture including the crowd of boys and men which had gathered.

"Yes, we are! we are!" eagerly shouted Ctesippus, a devoted friend of Cleinias. Others enthusiastically repeated his cry. "O

Euthydemus and Dionysodorus," said Socrates, rolling the two long names off his tongue in an impressively respectful way, "what you are about to undertake is no small task. But tell me first, if you will be so kind, can you make a man excellent only if he is *convinced* that he ought to learn from you, or even if he thinks that excellence cannot be taught at all."

"Even so, Socrates."

"Then let us hear you convince Cleinias that he ought to seek for wisdom and learn from you two brothers how to excel."

"We'll do this at once," Euthydemus proclaimed boldly, "if he is willing to answer questions."

"He's used to that," Socrates assured them, "when he and his friends get involved in an argument."

"Good!" said the sophist. Then, solemnly assuming an air of great authority, he began, "First you must tell me, Cleinias, what kind of people learn. Are they the clever or the dull?"

Overpowered by his portentous manner, the lad blushed. He looked toward Socrates, who saw he was embarrassed, and said, "Don't be afraid, Cleinias, just say whatever you think."

Dionysodorus, sitting on the other side of Socrates, whispered proudly to him, "Whichever he says, my brother will prove him wrong."

Cleinias answered, "The clever are the ones who learn."

"You had teachers in school, I suppose? teachers of reading and of how to play the lyre?"

"Of course."

"While you were still learning, did you yet know how to do these things?"

"No."

"You were still ignorant?"

"We were."

"Therefore the ignorant learn, not the clever or wise. Your first answer was wrong," Euthydemus proclaimed triumphantly.

The admirers of the sophists burst into loud laughter and applause.

Giving Cleinias no time to collect his thoughts, Dionysodorus broke in, "But tell me this. When the teacher dictated something, was it the ignorant who wrote it down correctly, or the clever?"

"The clever."

"Then the clever do learn. You have given a second wrong answer."

Cleinias looked confused—the effect the sophist had intended to produce.

The brothers continued to take turns in this way, always using expressions that had two common implications, and assuming whichever differed from what Cleinias had understood. It was as if they had been playing ball, Socrates declared afterward. Each brother caught the ball the other threw, and aimed it so as to hit Cleinias. The crowd of followers applauded with more enthusiasm every time.

At last Socrates decided to put an end to their treating the youth so unfairly. To avoid angering the sophists, who had become more proud at each burst of applause, Socrates resorted to what his friends called his characteristic "Socratic irony." He flattered the brothers a little, while declaring his own lack of skill.

"These sophists, Cleinias," he said, "are only playing tricks with words for a joke. Later they will show you their great wisdom. One of our most common Greek words (*manthanein*) can be used meaning to *acquire knowledge* about that of which one was ignorant. But it can also be used to mean the act of one who has this knowledge and applies it to some speech or action: who *understands*. By not explaining which they had in mind, they played a trick on you, as a boy might pull away the stool on which another was about to sit, then laugh when his surprised playmate fell sprawling on the floor."

Then Socrates offered to give the brothers an example of the serious type of questioning with which he wished them to instruct Cleinias. "You two men," he said, "may think my way of questioning far from expert, even ridiculous, but please remember I am only using it in order to bring you to the point of revealing your wisdom.

"All men," Socrates began, "want to get along well, Cleinias, don't they? Perhaps that is too absurd a question to ask, for there is surely no one who doesn't, is there?"

"No, no one."

"What does getting along well imply? having much that is good?"

The lad agreed.

"What sort of things is it good to have? we don't need a wise man to tell us, for everybody would say money, for one."

"Yes, indeed."

"And then he would add health and a good appearance."

"Of course."

"What else is it good to have? How about such qualities as courage and a sense of justice and also self-mastery? Some people might question our including these, but what do you think?"

"They are certainly good things to have."

"Shall we class knowledge also among the good things?"

"Among them surely."

"Have we now included everything important?"

"I think we have."

"No, by Zeus! We have forgotten something most important."

"What is it, Socrates?"

"Good fortune. All people, even the least intelligent, will say it is essential."

"That's true."

"Wait a moment, Cleinias. We are just about to make ourselves ridiculous before all these listeners." (It is significant that he said "we" instead of "you.")

"Why do you say that?"

"We shall be repeating—saying the same thing twice."

"How do you mean?"

"We have already included knowledge, Cleinias, and knowledge is in itself good fortune. Even a child could recognize that."

Socrates saw that the young man was surprised and puzzled, so he continued, "Aren't you aware that when it is a question of flute-playing, those who are most successful and have the best fortune are the ones who have the most knowledge of the instrument?"

Socrates then went on to give other examples. At sea, the most fortunate pilots are those who know most. When a soldier, one would prefer to follow a general with superior knowledge rather than one who was ignorant. When sick, one would try to get a doctor distinguished for his knowledge. One would be more fortunate in action when acting with a man who had knowledge instead of proceeding with one who was ignorant. Summing up, Socrates said, "We agree then that if knowledge is present, one doesn't need anything more in order to win success and have good fortune."

Socrates next suggested that they reconsider the statement with which they started their discussion, that a man would be happy if he possessed certain good things. Something more than mere possession, he now said, would be needed. The good things must be used and used rightly. One would not be better off for merely owning food without eating. A carpenter might possess every kind of tool, but if he was to gain good fortune and happiness, he must use them, and use them rightly. To do this, he would need knowledge.

"Do you not think then, Cleinias," said Socrates," that each of us should try to acquire all the knowledge he possibly can, truly loving it and seeking it always?"

"Yes, Socrates, and I will seek it with all my might."

After giving this fine example of a type of questioning that could lead to a desire for wisdom, Socrates asked the brothers to take up the subject where he left off, even suggesting that they show Cleinias whether he should strive to gain all knowledge, or whether there might be one certain kind that would make him good and happy, and what that kind was.

They paid no attention to this, but continued their favorite procedure of playing tricks with words. Socrates was disappointed to see that all the listeners, except Cleinias and himself, enjoyed this meaningless trickery.

"Tell me, Socrates," said Dionysodorus, "when you claimed you wanted Cleinias to gain knowledge, were you speaking in fun or in earnest?"

"In profound earnest."

"Think carefully, Socrates. You may have to deny your words."

"I have thought. I will never deny them."

"You wish him to become wise?"

"I certainly do."

"Is he now wise?"

"He says he is not, for he would not boast."

"Therefore you wish him to be what he is not, that is to be no longer what he is. You wish him not to be—that is, to die. A fine thing for a friend to wish!"

Ctesippus, who was devoted to Cleinias, broke in. "What makes you tell such a lie? If Zeus were not the protector of strangers in cities where they were not born, I would invoke him to destroy you for the lie you have told."

Euthydemus intervened. "Do you think, Ctesippus, that it is possible to tell a lie?"

"By Zeus! I do. Otherwise I should be insane."

The brothers then took turns in refuting Ctesippus, reaching the lowest level of absurdity in a way that caused Socrates to say, "Euthydemus, I may be too dull to understand your subtleties, but I wish to ask you a question. If there is no such thing as error in action or word or thought, as you claim, what did you come to Athens to teach? Didn't you say that you could teach excellence in the best possible way?"

The other brother asked indignantly, "Are you such an old fool, Socrates, that you bring up what was said before in order to evade a refutation? Next you will probably bring up something I said a year ago."

"It is difficult to answer when I do not understand the sense of words, that is with what meaning you are using them."

"Are the things that have sense of feeling alive, Socrates, or lifeless?"

"Alive."

"Do you know any word that is alive?"

"No, I don't."

"Then why did you want to know what sense my words had?"

"Perhaps because I made a mistake—and yet, perhaps I did not. If I did make a mistake and you do not refute it, wise as you are, then your wisdom has failed. But if I did make a mistake, you are wrong in saying that there is no such thing as error—and this statement you made less than a year ago. I am inclined to think, Euthydemus and Dionysodorus, that this argument is not likely to make any progress, for even your astonishing skill in the subtleties of logic has not found a way to overthrow another person without falling down yourself."

Ctesippus exclaimed, "I'm surprised at you, Dionysodorus and Euthydemus. You seem to have no objection at all to talking nonsense."

Socrates tried to prevent a real quarrel by checking Ctesippus, saying, as he had to Cleinias, that the sophists were only playing tricks and would later become serious. He then changed the subject to a consideration of what philosophy was, questioning Cleinias. When he saw the sophists were no longer angry, he drew them into the discussion again.

This led to even more quibbles on a still lower level. In the course of it Dionysodorus asked Ctesippus if he had a dog.

"Yes, indeed, and he's no good," was the answer.

"Has he any puppies?"

"Yes, and they're just as useless as he is."

"You know the dog is their father?"

"He certainly is."

"The dog is a father and he is yours, therefore he is your father, and the puppies are your brothers."

This was followed by the loudest applause of all.

When Socrates told his lifelong friend Crito about this occasion, the latter agreed with him that while a few persons might approve of the foolish arguments of these sophists, the majority would be more ashamed to use such methods than to be refuted by them. He also remarked that a respected speech-writer who had listened to the brothers informed him that they talked nonsense. This was Crito's opinion as well, but he was troubled because the same man declared to him that philosophy was ridiculous.

"I am anxious about my elder son, Socrates," he said. "He is just old enough to begin thoughtful study. But when I listen to any of those who train the mind, they seem to me so unreasonable that I hesitate to turn the lad toward philosophy."

"Dear Crito," Socrates replied, "don't you know that in every profession the inferior persons are numerous and negligible, while the excellent are few, but deserve high esteem? Don't trouble yourself about the teachers. Think of philosophy itself. After you have examined it thoroughly, if you have found it worthless, turn not only your son, but everyone else, away from it. But if you find it is what I believe it to be, take heart. Confidently seek and practise it, you and your entire family."

5 / In battle for the mind of a young man

Early one morning, long before daylight, Socrates was awakened by loud thumps on his front door. Somebody in the house opened it. The next moment the visitor rushed in, shouting, "Socrates, are you awake or still asleep?"

Recognizing the young man's voice, Socrates called out, "Why, Hippocrates! I hope nothing serious has happened?"

"The best thing possible!" his friend exclaimed. "Protagoras has come to Athens!"

"Day before yesterday," said Socrates. "Have you just heard?"

"Late last night," Hippocrates answered, feeling in the dark for a place on the bed near the feet of Socrates, where he seated himself. "I had been out in the country all day, and it wasn't until just as we were going to bed that my brother told me. I wanted to come to you right away, but he insisted it was too late. Of course, as soon as I woke up, I couldn't wait a moment longer. I

simply must catch Protagoras while he is still in, and I need
your help."

Socrates, who often teased a little, asked, "Why are you in such
a hurry? Has Protagoras committed a crime against you, so you
want to take him to court?"

The young man laughed. "That's just it," he replied. "He is
wonderfully wise, but hasn't even begun to make me so."

"He will if you pay his fee."

"I hope that's all that's needed," Hippocrates joyfully exclaimed. "I'll give him all the money I have, and all I can get from
my friends. Let's go at once. He's staying at the house of Callias.
When he came before, I was a child. Now you can recommend
me to him as a pupil. Come along!"

Socrates understood that the young man was too excited to be
told to wait, or even to remain seated. "I'll get up," he said, "and
we'll walk around in the courtyard and talk until it's light. Then
we'll go."

Socrates took advantage of this opportunity to prevent his
young friend, if he could, from being thoughtlessly dazzled by
the popular sophist. Evidently Hippocrates had been swept away
by the enthusiasm of friends of his own age and was ready to join
them in excitement and unthinking admiration. Would it be possible to induce him to reflect? Socrates could make the effort at
least. Too many Athenians were accepting and repeating state-

ments that sounded authoritative, but when carefully examined were proved only to bewilder by superficial cleverness.

In his usual way, Socrates began with a question. "If, instead of going to Protagoras, you were now going to the celebrated doctor, whose name is yours as well, Hippocrates, and were prepared to pay him any amount for his teaching, what would you be hoping to become?"

"A doctor, I suppose."

"What is the profession in which Protagoras is famous?"

"They call him a sophist."

"But you surely aren't looking forward to presenting yourself to the Greek world as another sophist?"

"No, indeed, Socrates, I should be ashamed to do that," he said, thinking of the high fees they charged. He belonged to an aristocratic family in Athens, none of whose members would expect to charge a fee for any service they might render.

Seeing that the young man was at a loss, Socrates led his thought in another direction. This considerate guidance signaled how different his method was from that of Euthydemus.

"Perhaps we should not consider the teaching of Protagoras," he said, "in the same category as the work of a doctor. It may hold such a place as the instruction you received in school from the teachers of reading and lyre-playing and athletics. You were learning not in order to teach those branches yourself, but to gain the knowledge needed by a free citizen of Athens. Such things are part of a liberal education."

"That's it exactly," said Hippocrates, much relieved.

"Do you fully realize, my friend, what you are about to do? You are going to accept in your own mind the instruction of a sophist. And yet I am inclined to think that you do not know just what a sophist is. If you don't, it is impossible for you to know whether the result will be good for you or bad."

"But I think I do know."

"Tell me then. What do you think a sophist is?"

"As the word indicates, he is one who knows."

"Can't that be said just as readily even of carpenters? They know about carpentry. About what does a sophist have knowledge?"

"What should we say, Socrates? Wouldn't it be knowledge of how to make a man speak well?"

"That may be true, but it is not definite enough, for the answer at once prompts another question. To make a man speak well about what? Wouldn't it have to be about something the sophist understands?"

"By Zeus, Socrates, you were right! I can't tell you that."

"Do you see then to what danger you are about to submit your mind and soul? You would not submit your body for treatment to a doctor you did not know, without first consulting others whose opinion you could trust. In the evening you heard that this foreigner had come to Athens. The next morning you hurry to go to him and pay any amount for him to instruct you. You do not know him, you have not asked anyone about him. You call him a sophist, but you cannot tell what a sophist is. Yet you are ready to entrust your mind and soul to him."

"That is how it seems," Hippocrates said regretfully.

Again Socrates led him a step farther.

"Isn't a sophist a man who sells food by which the mind may be nourished?"

"What nourishes the mind, Socrates?"

"Knowledge, of course. And just as in the case of food for the body, we must be careful about what we buy. For those who sell food for the mind are like those who sell food for the body, either retail or wholesale. They praise all that they have to sell without positively knowing whether it will be good for the person they are persuading or not. In fact, we should be more careful in buying food for the mind, for we cannot carry it away in a bag. In order to take it away, we must receive it in our own minds, making it a part of us, being benefited if it is truly good, but harmed if it is bad. If you fully understand what is good and what is bad for the mind to make a part of itself, then you can safely listen to Protagoras or any other sophist, rejecting at once what is not good. Otherwise his praise of what he is teaching may deceive you, leading you to plant deep in your mind what will harm you greatly.

"Since it is light now," Socrates continued, "let us go to hear Protagoras. After we have heard what he has to say, we can talk it over with each other and with some of the distinguished men who are also guests of Callias."

On the way they began to talk about another subject. Because they had not come to a definite decision by the time they reached their destination, the young man would not let Socrates knock at once, but insisted they should go on talking in the vestibule until they worked their way to a real conclusion.

This youth, who had been so eager to get to Protagoras that he could not wait for daylight, was now so absorbed in the new vistas of thought opened to him by Socrates that he would not miss any part. Socrates knew from this that his young friend was no longer in danger of being so excited by all he had heard about Protagoras as to be unable to test by thoughtful reasoning any claim the sophist might make.

The doorkeeper had apparently heard them talking, for when they knocked at last, he opened the door just a little, exclaimed, "More sophists! Master has no time for you," then slammed the door shut.

Knocking again, Socrates told the man they were not sophists and would not trouble Callias, but wanted to speak with Protagoras. Reluctantly the servant held the door open. While Socrates was protesting, Alcibiades and Critias had arrived, and now managed to slip in behind him without a word.

The reason for the servant's crustiness was at once apparent. Though this house was one of the largest in Athens, there seemed to be enough people crowded into it to have filled a marketplace. Different voices could be heard, causing the young man to remember what Socrates had said about sophists praising what they had to offer prospective students, much as rival dealers in a market praised their wares.

Three of the most respected sophists were staying as guests of Callias, who had welcomed with each a number of friends traveling with him on his lecture tour. Socrates did not wonder that the doorkeeper had tried to let no more enter. Callias had assigned to each renowned sophist a place where he could lecture to his own group without being disturbed. Each group included, as well as the foreigners, some Athenians who were eager to form their own opinions about men they had heard extravagantly praised.

Protagoras was walking back and forth in the courtyard, lecturing, while his listeners followed in reverential silence. Socrates thought that not even the mythical Orpheus could have held men more entranced. It amused him to see how careful everyone was to keep the great man always in front. There were two on each side of him, making a front line of five. The others formed orderly rows behind. When he came to the end of the court, Protagoras turned. At once those following parted, forming a line on each side. Protagoras led his line between these until it was again first, with the rest filling in behind. This was done as smoothly as if they had been trained in a theater to keep the leading actor in his place of honor.

At a distance from this orderly procession, the less energetic sophist Hippias had been provided with a throne-like chair. Before it were benches filled with admirers who asked questions about the original substance from which all others developed. Was the one that first existed earth, or air, or water, or something else? He answered without hesitation in an authoritative manner.

The third sophist, Prodicus, had completely avoided exertion by remaining in bed, under a heap of warm fleeces. The bed had been moved into what was previously used as a store-room, but was cleared when the house became so full of guests. Chairs for listeners filled it to the walls, and the sophist's deep voice could be heard far down the hall.

When Protagoras had apparently reached a conclusion, Socrates stepped up to him and introduced his young friend. The sophist greeted both, asking if they wanted to speak with him alone or before others.

"Whichever you prefer," said Socrates, "after you learn why we have come. Hippocrates belongs to an important wealthy family in Athens, and no lad of his age has shown more ability. He would like to enter political life, and he believes he could do this most successfully by receiving instruction from you. Tell me, please, whether you would rather talk to us alone or not."

In reply, Protagoras, always eager to make a long speech, seized the opportunity. He claimed that the art of a sophist was an ancient one, practiced by many whose names had become great under some other designation. Such men classed themselves among the poets, or another honored group, in order to escape envy or slander. But he himself scorned such evasion. He acknowledged that he was a sophist and a teacher.

"I have done this for many years," he said, "with no bad results, and I am old enough to be the father of anyone I see here. I should prefer to hold our talk in the presence of others."

Socrates saw that Protagoras wanted as many as possible to

know that this young man of outstanding ability had selected him for a teacher, so he suggested, "Then why don't we invite Prodicus and Hippias to join us, bringing their groups?"

"By all means," said Protagoras, obviously delighted.

Callias, their host, was pleased as well. "Shall we all unite then," he asked, "and carry on a discussion together?"

This won general aproval. It meant that nobody would miss what one sophist had to say while listening to another. More benches and chairs were moved to where the followers of Hippias were gathered, while Callias and Alcibiades (the latter always eager to be at the center of any action) went to pull Prodicus out of bed.

But Socrates did not say what Protagoras wanted the assembled crowd to hear. He was pleased to have the other sophists listen while Protagoras described his method of teaching, and perhaps contribute to the discussion, but he did not intend to flatter the older sophist by implying that he had been chosen in preference to them. If this disappointed Protagoras, he could do nothing about it.

· Socrates said, "I will begin as I did before. Hippocrates would like to become your pupil. He wants to know what will happen to him if he does."

"Young man," the sophist declared, "on the very first day that you are with me, you will go home a better man. On the next, the same thing will happen again, and on each following day you will continue to improve."

After he had made this imposing claim, Protagoras must have been amazed to hear Socrates say, "This is not at all remarkable. Advanced in years and renowned as you are, Protagoras, for wisdom," (so Socrates tried to lessen the shock), "if anyone were to teach you what you did not happen to know, you would improve. Please tell me how and in regard to what he will improve."

"That is a good question," said Protagoras, ignoring what had preceded, "and I enjoy answering good questions." Then, in his usual way, he took advantage of a chance to amplify his answer.

"By coming to me," he said, "Hippocrates will not be forced to undergo what another sophist would have imposed upon him. The others misuse the young men who come expecting to have escaped at last from geometry and astronomy and music, and at once they find themselves thrust back into those studies. But when they come to me, they learn only what they hoped to acquire—good judgment about their own affairs, in order to manage their homes well, and good judgment about the affairs of the city, so as to be expert in managing them and in giving advice."

"Do I follow you?" Socrates asked. "It seems to me that you teach skill in politics and promise to make men good citizens."

"You are exactly right," Protagoras answered. "That is my profession."

"Certainly a fine skill to have acquired—if you really have. I used to think this could not be taught. But since you make the statement so positively, I admit I do not feel quite sure. Let me tell you why I thought so."

Socrates then called attention to two facts. In the Athenian assembly, when it met to debate a matter requiring knowledge in some special field—for instance, the erection of buildings or the construction of ships—an expert was called in to give advice. This would be a man who knew more about the subject than the average citizen. He had acquired knowledge partly from being taught by more advanced professionals and partly from actual experience. When, however, the question was about city affairs, any citizen was allowed to speak and the assembly considered his advice. There were, of course, public men whose advice had helped the city in the past, but most of them were apparently not able to teach their sons to develop the ability they themselves possessed.

"When I think of these things," Socrates said, "I am inclined to believe that this kind of excellence cannot be taught. But now that I have heard you say it can, I wish you would prove this to me more clearly. You have wide experience, I know. You have learned many things, and yourself discovered much. I beg that you will reveal some of this to me, especially what you consider a definite proof that excellence can be taught. I can name many persons who are excellent themselves, but have never caused anyone else to improve, either within their own families or outside of them."

"I will do this gladly," Protagoras replied. "Would you rather have me explain it in the form of a myth or by process of reasoning?"

When many expressed their desire that he should make the choice, he said he thought the myth would be more interesting.

Although Socrates preferred proof by reasoning, he raised no objection.

Protagoras then delivered a long speech. He began with the creation of men and animals, and proceeded to the gathering of men in cities. Since at first they had no knowledge of government, they soon began to injure one another. Zeus, fearing that this would lead to the destruction of the entire human race, sent his messenger, Hermes, to implant justice and reverence in the hearts of all men. Some degree of each is essential to establish order and develop friendliness in a community.

"This, Socrates," said Protagoras, "is the reason why every citizen is granted the right to speak in the Athenian assembly. It is assumed that everyone has some understanding of justice and also some power of self-restraint, so as to adjust his actions in accord with it."

Without pausing for a moment, Protagoras next took up in detail the subject of instruction as to what is right and what is wrong. This, he declared, began in the first years of childhood and continued to the end of life, for the state compelled the mature citizen to learn the laws and obey them. Justice and self-control were constantly being taught in various ways, everyone being ready to teach justice according to his own ability. But not all who were being taught had the same natural capacity and desire to learn. That explained why some were inferior to their fathers. "If anyone was able to make others advance even a little in excellence, we should be content. I think that I am a teacher of this kind, particularly able to help anyone become all that a man should be."

After a few complimentary remarks, Socrates said there was one thing that still troubled him, so he would like to ask the sophist a question. He then added another compliment, saying he knew Protagoras was able to answer questions. Some eloquent speakers, on the other hand, would not give a brief, clear answer. They insisted on making another extended speech, just as brazen pots, when struck, go on resounding and will not stop till you put your hand on them.

"While you were speaking, Protagoras," he said, "you sometimes mentioned justice, self-control, and right action as if together they constituted excellence. What I wish to ask is: are these different names for the same thing? or are they names for different parts of excellence, each with a different function, as the nose and mouth are different parts of the face?"

"They are names for different parts of excellence."

"If a man has one part, must he have all the others?"

"By no means. Many men are grave, but not just, and many are just, but not wise."

"Then you think courage and wisdom are also parts of excellence?"

"Undoubtedly."

They proceeded in this way for some time. But suddenly, in answer to a question of Socrates, Protagoras made a speech of some length. At the end of it, the listeners shouted their admiration as they applauded.

Seeing that the sophist did not wish to continue giving short answers, Socrates rose to leave, but Callias seized him, saying, "I simply will not let you go. We want to hear you and Protagoras go on."

Socrates protested, with an apology, that he lacked the ability to follow a long speech.

"But don't you see," Callias asked, "that Protagoras has as much right to speak in his way as you have to keep to your method?"

Young Alcibiades interrupted, "No, Callias, you are wrong. Socrates admits he cannot make a speech. And we have all heard how Protagoras can. But Protagoras claims to be just as able to answer briefly. He ought to do this now."

Seeing that all wanted the discussion resumed, Socrates suggested that they should take turns, with Protagoras first questioning him.

Protagoras then quoted from a poem by Simonides, after declaring that he thought the most important part of education was to learn to recognize in a poem what parts of it are correct, and which are not, always giving reasons to support his judgment. "If two statements in the same poem are contradictory," he said, "then it has not been well composed. Now, listen to this." He quoted again. The audience laughed and applauded.

This led Socrates to show that he could outdo the sophists in their own field, while applying their own method. His reasoning was perverse, in ways the sophists enjoyed, making it a brilliant caricature, yet at the same time cleverly introducing a positive conviction of Socrates—the belief that excellence is attained by knowledge.

After this amusing interlude, Socrates led to the consideration of what was being debated before the quotation was introduced by the sophist.

"You said, Protagoras, if I remember correctly, that wisdom, self-control, courage, justice, and right action are all parts of excellence, but each is separate from the others and has a different function, similar to the different parts of the face."

Protagoras recalled what he had admitted previously, that three of them—justice, self-control, and right action—are to some extent related to wisdom, since without its aid they could not be brought into action. But he declared he still believed that many men were ignorant, unjust, and impetuous, but remarkably courageous.

Socrates, by the short questions that he thought would best clarify a subject, brought the argument to a point where Protagoras admitted defeat.

"Finish the argument by yourself," he said. "Since you want an answer, I will say that, consistently with our argument, it seems impossible to maintain my statement."

Socrates responded with equal courtesy. "Each of us," he said, "has shifted his attitude since the beginning of our talk. I, who believed that excellence could not be taught, find myself trying to prove that knowledge is essential to each form of excellence, and knowledge can be taught. On the other hand, you, who said it could be taught, now declare that a person who is ignorant can possess one of the forms of excellence. I should like to have your help in carrying this inquiry further."

Protagoras replied: "I praise your enthusiasm, Socrates, and I admire the way you conduct an argument. I have already said to many that I think far more highly of you than of anyone else of your age I have met. Indeed, I believe that you are going to become eminent in philosophy. I shall be glad to continue this discussion with you whenever you wish."

Listening carefully, Hippocrates had the experience of hearing the sophist he had believed to be extraordinary not only defeated by Socrates, but more than ready to talk with him again.

6/ *The winning-over*

The sophist Thrasymachus took pride in his power to overcome an opponent. In an encounter with Socrates, however, he had a disturbing experience. The philosopher's clear thinking and superior logic exposed the sophist's bombastic pretense. He had not enough acuteness to see where Socrates was leading the argument before it defeated him. This occurred in the house of Polemarchus on an evening made memorable by one of Plato's *Dialogues,* the *Republic.*

When Socrates was about fifty, he walked one day with Glaucon down to Piraeus, then as now the harbor of Athens. They went to see the celebration of a festival in honor of the goddess Bendis, whose worship was being introduced from Thrace. A fine procession had been organized by the people of Piraeus, but that of the Thracian visitors was no less splendid. As Socrates and his young companion were starting to walk back to Athens, they were stopped by a group in which they found Glaucon's brother, Adeimantus. (The youngest brother of these two was Plato, then a boy no more than seven.)

Socrates was surprised to feel someone behind pulling his mantle. Turning, he saw the slave-boy of Polemarchus, who said, "My master wants you to wait."

"Where is he?" Socrates asked.

"Just a little way behind. He told me to run and stop you. He'll soon catch up. Do wait!"

45

"We will, of course," said Glaucon.

Polemarchus, arriving with his group, inquired, with a laugh, "Socrates, are you and Glaucon starting back to the city?"

"As you've guessed."

"Do you see how many of us there are?"

"Of course."

Still laughing, Polemarchus declared, "You'll have to fight every one of us, if you don't consent to stay here."

"Might we not persuade you," Socrates asked, "that you ought to let us go?"

"Could you persuade people who wouldn't listen?"

"Of course not," said Glaucon, also laughing.

"That's exactly what is going to happen," Polemarchus proclaimed.

"Didn't you know," Adeimantus asked excitedly, "that in the

evening there is going to be a torch-race on horseback in honor
of the goddess?"

"On horseback!" Socrates was surprised. "That is certainly
something new. Will they actually pass torches to one another
while riding?"

"They will indeed," said Polemarchus, "and besides that, there
will be a late night festival well worth seeing. Come home with
me to dinner. Afterward we'll enjoy going out to watch what
happens."

Polemarchus led them all to his house, where they found his
brothers and their father, Cephalus, with a few friends, including
the sophist Thrasymachus.

Socrates was startled to see how Cephalus had aged since the
last time they had met. He now looked very old, but he called out
warmly.

"Socrates, how glad I am to see you! You don't come here to
Piraeus as often as you should. Now that I can't get to Athens
easily, you really ought to make a point of coming more. Since
I've had to limit my activities, there is nothing I enjoy so much
as good talk. Do remember to come here every little while to see
me and my sons."

"There is something I would like to learn from you, Cephalus,"
said Socrates. "Have you found life become harder in your
old age?"

"No, indeed," he replied. "I'll tell you how I feel about it. Some
of my friends often complain, when we get together, about how
they miss their former enjoyment of the pleasures of youth. Now,
they lament, they don't feel really alive any more. But they are
wrong to blame old age for this, as the cause is in themselves. I
am relieved by a sense of peace and freedom, now that I am no
longer subject to violent passionate desires."

"I understand," said Socrates, "but I suspect that many will not
believe you feel this because of old age. They will say it is because you are so rich that you are so contented."

"You're right. They do say that. And there is something in it,
of course. Old age is not easy for a poor man. But it is equally true
that no amount of wealth makes it easy for a rich man who is not
at peace with himself."

"Tell me, if you will, what you consider the greatest good that
your wealth has given you."

"Wealth can keep a man of character from being tempted to

deceive or injure others, or to neglect his debts to gods or men. And when we feel that death can no longer be far away, we begin to recall what we have heard about punishment of the dead for sins committed in life. Some unjust men who have never thought of this before are even tortured by dread."

"But is justice then no more than telling the truth and paying one's debts?" Socrates asked.

So began a discussion that lasted a great part of the night, causing the interested participants to forget all about the festival they had expected to attend. It fills the ten "books" of Plato's *Republic* and consists mostly of attempts by Glaucon and Adeimantus, with the help of Socrates, to completely define the nature of justice.

Socrates, whose imagination moved quickly, at once suggested a case in which it would not be right to return someone's property. If a man borrowed a friend's weapon, and the friend later became insane and then demanded it, no one would think it right for it to be given back. Exceptional as this would be, it proved that the definition of justice was not conclusive, as Cephalus agreed.

"Yet it is generally a correct definition," Polemarchus protested, "at least, if we believe the poet Simonides."

Just then Cephalus was called away to attend to some sacrifices. But first, with a smile, he said he bequeathed the argument to his son and heir. Polemarchus then quoted the saying of Simonides that what was borrowed should be returned.

"I should not like to contradict Simonides," declared Socrates, "for he was an inspired poet. Yet I am very sure that he did not mean to include such a situation as I mentioned."

"I too feel he didn't," Polemarchus assented, "for Simonides said somewhere else that it was right to help friends and never harm them."

The duty to help friends and harm enemies was a widely accepted part of conventional morality at this time. By questioning the young man in detail, with various illustrations, Socrates led him finally to admit that no one who willfully injured another could be called just.

"Then we must not assume that such an idea was implied by Simonides," said Socrates.

"I agree," Polemarchus replied.

"Would you like to know who in my opinion must have originated the familiar saying that it is right to help friends and harm enemies?" Socrates then asked.

"Who?"

"I think it was some tyrant or other rich and mighty man who was proud of his power. Now let us search for a better definition of justice."

Thrasymachus, the sophist, had tried to interrupt several times, but others held him back. Now that there was a pause, he burst in like a wild beast leaping upon its prey.

"You are fools, you two!" he roared. "Why does each of you lie down and let the other walk over him? If you want to know what justice really is, don't ask questions and pride yourself on refuting the answers. To answer is much harder than to ask. Now, Socrates, you answer me. Tell me what you claim justice is. And don't say it is necessary or beneficial or advantageous. Speak more precisely. I will not accept such vague stuff as has been satisfying you."

"Don't be angry with me," gently protested Socrates. "If we went astray in our argument, it was unintentional. You would not accuse us if we were seeking for gold. We are trying to find justice, a thing far more precious than gold. Remember this, my friend. But so far, it seems, we are unable to discover it. You others who are more clever should feel pity for us, not anger."

With a bitter laugh, the sophist exclaimed, "The irony of Socrates, as usual! Didn't I tell you all that he would not be willing to answer, but would do everything to avoid that? What if I give you a better definition of justice, Socrates, than any of you have been considering? Then what will you deserve?"

"The penalty of ignorance. To be taught by one who knows."

"You are a simpleton! Do you expect to be taught without paying?"

"When I have the money, I will pay," Socrates said.

"You have it already," Glaucon interposed. "And you, Thrasymachus, need have no anxiety about payment. We will all contribute for Socrates."

"Yes, and I know why you will," the sophist declared angrily. "Because you want to hear Socrates do what he always does— avoid answering, but take up the answer of someone else and tear it apart."

"My friend," said Socrates quietly, "How could I answer, when

I do not know? You, however, Thrasymachus, claim that you do know and are able to give a convincing definition. I beg that you will tell what it is. Don't keep it from us."

When all the rest expressed eagerness to hear the sophist's definition, Thrasymachus pretended to be reluctant, though it was obvious to everyone that he was wanting to be urged. At last he consented.

"This is the way of Socrates," he said, "he refuses to teach, but goes around learning from others and never even thanks them."

"It is true that I learn from others," said Socrates, "but I am not ungrateful. I pay as much as I can. Since I have no money, all I can often give in return is praise, and this I give readily when anyone speaks well, as you soon may see."

"Listen then. I maintain that justice is whatever benefits the stronger person."

All were silent.

"Well, why don't you praise me, Socrates?"

"I need to know first exactly what you mean. You cannot possibly believe that because a wrestler finds it benefits him to eat beef, it would help us."

"That is ridiculous!" Thrasymachus shouted angrily, "You are giving that meaning to my words, just in order to destroy the argument."

So many sophists and their admirers were showing off in exactly this way that people had the habit of expecting it, with the result that frequently they failed to understand Socrates. His aim was constantly to clarify the thought of himself and all who talked with him, in the hope that they might finally reach an agreement.

To make it evident that he was far from feeling any personal hostility, he said in a warmly genial tone, "My friend, that is not my intention. Do make your statement more clear."

The sophist then referred to different forms of government, of which the two extremes are democracy and tyranny. Each form, including all between, makes laws, he declared, to secure its own advantage. It also punishes any who break them, for it has the power and is stronger.

A long discussion followed, beginning with the question of Socrates, "Does the governing power, whether one man or more, ever make a mistake? Does it, while intending to secure its own advantage, establish a law that does not bring it benefit? Since you have already stated that the subjects are weaker and must obey the laws, then the rulers will be compelling the subjects to do what will injure the rulers, so bringing about the opposite of their advantage."

Polemarchus, unable to remain silent, said positively, "Nothing could be clearer, Socrates."

But someone objected, "Only, Polemarchus, if he takes you as witness."

"There is no need of any witness," Polemarchus retorted. "Thrasymachus has already said that for subjects to obey the ruling power is justice. If this power unintentionally commands what will injure it, justice will be an injury of the ruling power instead of its advantage."

The other persisted, "He meant what the stronger power *thought* would be to its advantage."

Polemarchus insisted, "That was not the statement he made."

Socrates smiled. "Never mind," he said. "Let us accept the new statement, if Thrasymachus has changed his opinion."

Socrates was always ready to accept such a change on the part of anyone participating in the argument, and to shift to an examination of the new statement. His aim was to arrive at truth, if possible.

"Did you wish, Thrasymachus," he asked, "to say that justice was what the stronger thought to be his advantage, whether it really was or not?"

"No, indeed," was the contemptuous reply. "Do you think I call a man strong who is mistaken?"

"I thought you meant that when you said a ruler might be mistaken."

"You are a cheat, Socrates," the sophist declared indignantly. "In what he is mistaken about, he is not a ruler in the precise sense I require. A physician, if he is mistaken about a sick man, is not at that moment truly a physician, a healer."

"Do you really think I am trying to cheat you?" Socrates asked.

"I positively know you are."

"Do you believe I am intending to injure you by asking these questions?"

"Of course. I know you do. But your cheating won't get you anywhere."

"I would never attempt to cheat Thrasymachus," Socrates said, smiling. "Can you imagine I have so little sense as to try to shave a lion?"

The sophist refused to asume a lighter tone. "You just did try," he said rudely, "but you failed."

Socrates turned away from personalities. "Has the physician's art defects?" he asked. "I'll explain what I mean. A man's body has certain natural functions, but his eyes may be deficient in sight or his ears in hearing. Does the art itself, if it is true and perfect, ever need to be cured or corrected by something outside itself, as the parts of the body do?"

His opponent admitted it did not.

"Does the art ever try to gain any benefit for itself alone? Or is its sole aim to cure the patient by means of the knowledge of the true doctor?"

"That is all," he admitted, but most reluctantly.

"Then the true art of healing, the true art of the doctor, works only for the patient's advantage?"

By this time the listeners saw that the definition so proudly offered by the sophist had failed to stand the test. But Thrasymachus surprised everyone by suddenly asking, "Socrates, have you a nurse?"

Instead of being irritated, Socrates spoke calmly. "Why do you ask such a question?"

"Because she is not taking proper care of you," he said in an insulting tone. "She doesn't notice that your nose is running so badly that you can't see to tell a shepherd from his sheep."

The sophist then launched into a very long speech. He asserted that a shepherd tended his sheep for his own sake, not theirs, since he was planning to have them served as meat at his own table, or else to sell them at a market. Thrasymachus also introduced a point of view not previously considered by saying that whenever a just man became involved with an unjust one, the unjust man gained the advantage. If they were partners, the unjust one managed to obtain more. The same thing happened in their dealings with the state. When there was an income tax, the just man paid more and the unjust one less on the same amount of income. He concluded by declaring as impressively as an actor delivering an exit line, "Injustice, when on a sufficiently large scale, has more strength and mastery than justice. As I said before, justice is the advantage of the stronger man over others."

As he finished his long speech, he turned to leave, but was stopped by emphatic protests, in which Socrates joined.

"Why are you going?" he asked.

"Because I don't agree with you," said Thrasymachus scornfully.

"Would it not be better," Socrates asked with quiet courtesy, "to stay until you have taught us that your words are true, or perhaps have learned that they are not? Is the way a man's life should be lived so small a matter in your opinion that you do not wish to teach us what you say you know? Any wisdom you may be able to give so large a group as this will not be unrewarded. If an unjust man may be able to commit injustice by fraud or force, this fact does not convince me that injustice secures a greater advantage than justice, and some others may agree with me. Of course we could be wrong. If we are, you should show us that we are mistaken in preferring justice to injustice."

This convinced the sophist that Socrates was not prompted by malice or an intention to humiliate, but was friendly and sincere. He consented to remain, but he was completely at a loss as to how to proceed. He was not able to construct a logical argument, though he always made a speech consisting of positive assertions, unproved but highly seasoned with scorn of his opponent.

"What more can I say than I have just told you?" he asked. "Would you have me hammer my words into your minds?"

"No, not that," Socrates replied. "I would only ask you to be consistent; or, if you change your opinion, to do so frankly. When you defined the true physician, you did this in an exact sense, but you were not equally exact in defining the shepherd. His art requires only that he do what is best for the sheep, as the doctor's art requires that he do what is best for his patients. But you said the shepherd tended his sheep for his own gain, either as feaster or trader. You introduced the element of receiving pay. Yet I am sure you would not claim that the doctor's art is the art of receiving pay because he takes fees for his services."

"Certainly not."

"Then the payment is an additional advantage, but not an inseparable part of the art of healing. The payment is added because without it the doctor would not receive any benefit from his art."

The sophist gave a reluctant assent.

"For a similar reason," said Socrates, "men are not expected to undertake the duties of any of the lower government offices without being paid for doing so. No one wants to give his time and efforts for what is outside his own interests without being paid for it in some way. If the payment is not in money, it may be in honor, or even in escaping a penalty imposed for failing to do something thought necessary for the general welfare. I still believe that the true ruler is expected to make the welfare of his subjects his chief concern. But Thrasymachus declares that the life of the unjust man is more advantageous. With which of us do you agree, Glaucon?"

"With you, Socrates."

"Did you hear all the advantages of the unjust man that Thrasymachus enumerated?"

"Yes, I heard them, but I was not convinced."

"Would you like to convince him then, if we can find a way, that what he was saying was not true?"

"Indeed I would."

"If he makes a speech, which he prefers to do, and one of us replies in another speech, he will answer in still another speech, and we will have to reply to that, so we will certainly need judges to compare the arguments on both sides and determine which are to be accepted. But if we proceed by short steps and brief answers, never leaving a point till we two agree about it, we will need no other judges."

Glaucon preferred this, and Thrasymachus, seeing that the entire company felt the same way, consented to follow this method, which was called dialectic.

In that, he was far inferior to Socrates, but he made a desperate attempt, which caused perspiration to roll down his face and even drip on his garment. By logical steps Thrasymachus was compelled finally to admit that justice was both good and wise, while injustice was evil and ignorant. As he acknowleged this, all saw what no one had ever seen before. A fiery blush showed that the sophist was ashamed.

"Do you remember," Socrates asked, "that you made a different statement previously?"

"Of course I remember," he said impatiently, "and I am quite able to refute you. But in order to do this, I would have to make a speech, and it was decided that we should keep to dialectic. So go ahead now with your questions. I will not oppose you, for I see that would displease all these listeners."

Thrasymachus had yielded, but he had not changed his own opinion.

Many individuals in Athens were irritated, as this sophist was, by the way Socrates used dialectic, especially when they became involved in a discussion and found themselves guilty of a logical error. They might then leave, as Thrasymachus had started to do, feeling humiliated and disgusted. Those who avoided him thereafter often spread criticism of Socrates among other Athenians.

He was aware that this might happen, but nothing could cause him to swerve from the effort on which he had determined. He believed that the most important thing in life was to discover what was true and right, and to act accordingly. This would not come about by merely repeating what had been heard or read. It must result from careful individual thinking, if it was to be a reliable guide. Socrates also believed that the best way to arrive at this result was by serious discussion. Even a conversation ending in a negative result was not a waste of time, if it clarified some confusion or led to the discarding of false beliefs.

The number of persons who really learned from Socrates appears to have been large, and no more significant example than Thrasymachus can be found of one whose anger ended when he began to understand Socrates. He might not fully agree, but he no longer felt affronted.

As the argument proceeded in a more friendly fashion, Socrates asked, "If one state has acquired power over another, did it bring this about by justice or injustice?"

"If you are right in your view," the sophist answered, "that justice is wisdom, it must have been by justice. But if I am right, it was by injustice."

"I am delighted, Thrasymachus," Socrates said, "to have you give such an excellent answer."

The sophist was thinking of the injustice applied in overcoming its victim. Socrates, however, showed that the members of the conquering power would never have achieved this if they had not been just in their personal relations with one another. Otherwise they would never have accomplished anything.

The discussion then continued, Thrasymachus admitting the

logical steps in the development of the argument, but frequently interjecting such remarks as "I grant that because I don't want to quarrel with you," or "I will not oppose you, for that, I see, would displease these people."

Each time Socrates thanked him, then continued on the basis of the admission.

Finally he said, "Then, my dear Thrasymachus, injustice can never be more profitable than justice."

The sophist had admitted every step in the argument, but although he could not refute any point taken, he was unwilling to accept it fully. He no longer felt ill-will toward Socrates, but he was far from going all the way with him.

"Let this admission of mine," he said, "be the last morsel in your feast, Socrates, at the festival of Bendis."

"I thank you for it, Thrasymachus," Socrates replied, "since you have stopped being angry with me, and know I was never your enemy."

However, Socrates was not entirely satisfied, and this, he explained, was his own fault. "I am like a man at a feast," he said, "who eagerly tastes every dainty that is brought to the table before really savoring what preceded. Without discovering what justice is, I began to consider if it was good and wise or evil and foolish. And before I had completed that, I became interested in the comparative advantages of justice and injustice. The result is that I actually know nothing at all about justice, since I cannot truly say I know what it is."

So, with this revealing example of how Socrates could criticize his own argument, as well as those offered by others, the first book of Plato's *Republic* concludes. What follows, ending with the tenth book, starts with Glaucon's question, "Do you wish, Socrates, to convince us that it is always better to be just than unjust?"

"I certainly do," was the answer.

"That you have not yet done," Glaucon stated positively.

Many different things were taken up in the conversation that followed, notably the imagined construction of an ideal state. At the beginning of Book V, Socrates was about to consider forms of unjust government, when Adeimantus whispered to Polemarchus, ending with a question heard by all, "Shall we let it go?"

"Let what go?" inquired Socrates.

"You."

"Do tell me what you mean."

"We think you are lazily keeping from us a most interesting regulation of your imagined state. What is to be done about the women and children? What kind of family life will there be? Until you have explained that, we will not let you go on to another subject."

"I agree," added Glaucon.

"So do we all," said Thrasymachus. He was now no longer an opponent, but a member of the united group of listeners.

Then turning to Glaucon, Socrates said, "You do not perceive into what a swarm of difficulties you are forcing our discussion. I was avoiding it intentionally."

"But discussion is what we all enjoy," said Thrasymachus.

"True. But it should have a limit." Socrates smiled at the sophist, who now not only supported Socrates, but even wanted to hear him develop a subject longer than he had planned.

"Yet," said Glaucon, "the whole of life is not too much to devote to such discussion as this. We have agreed that the rulers of the state we are creating shall be a class of guardians, who shall make its interests their chief concern. They are to have no individual possessions, but among them all things will be shared. Tell us how there can be a sharing of family life."

"It is extremely difficult to explain," Socrates said, "for many doubts concerning it arise in my own mind. I am far from certain that sharing of family life is practicable. And if it could be contrived, I do not know whether it would be best."

After much urging, Socrates did consider the subject at some length. In consequence, especially as the study of "nuclear" and "extended" families has grown in interest, it has occasionally been mentioned in print that Socrates favored some kind of shared family life. But we should not forget that he prefaced the attempted explanation with these significant qualifications.

During the discussion, Socrates pointed out that women should be given the same education as men, and should hold equally high offices in the government; declaring that the intelligence of women is not less than that of men, and so should be given the same training.

This belief of Socrates was completely contrary to the long-established tradition which still prevailed in his time. Although the epic poetry of Homer gives a different picture of the life of women some centuries earlier, Athenians in the fifth century B.C. kept the women of their families secluded in the home.

The system was simple and rigid. Little girls were trained and taught by their mothers and any competent slave. Boys, as soon as they were seven, were separated from their sisters and put in the charge of a male slave, the *paidagogos*. He accompanied the boys to school, staying there to take them home, and teaching them to behave in all situations.

Girls meanwhile remained with the mother, who taught them all home duties in order to prepare them for marriage. Those duties included not only care of the house and preparation of food, but also spinning and weaving, since all the clothing of family and slaves was made in the home, and growing girls must learn to direct the slaves who performed these tasks.

When a girl was fifteen, her father chose a husband for her, usually a friend's son, about thirty years old. There was a formal betrothal ceremony at which the two were introduced. They met next at the wedding, after which they were escorted, often with singing, to what was to be their home. There they were left to get acquainted.

Socrates, it seems, married rather late in life. In the speech he made at his trial, he said that he had three sons—one in his teens, and both the others very small boys. At this time, Socrates himself was seventy. The youngest boy was so tiny that Xanthippe could not leave him at home, but had to bring him with her to the prison, where she was allowed to stay with Socrates the night before he was to die.

While the name of Socrates' wife came to be used proverbially, in both ancient and modern times, for a scolding woman, the definite contemporary information we have about her appears to be limited to three brief passages: one in the *Phaedo* of Plato (as mentioned in Chapter 12) and two taken from Xenophon.

In his *Memorabilia* (II.2.7-10), Xenophon tells of how Socrates reproved his oldest son, Lamprocles, for complaining that his mother criticized him, reminding the lad of how tenderly she had cared for him through his early years, and later whenever he became sick, in ways that proved enduring love.

In Xenophon's *Symposium* (II.8-9), Socrates declares that women are inferior to men only in physical strength and in the training received by them in Athens.

"Therefore," he continued, "let any man teach his wife whatever he desires."

"How is it then, Socrates," a fellow banqueter asked, "that you haven't trained Xanthippe? I think she is the hardest to get along with of all women who have ever lived—or ever will."

Socrates smiled. "Very early in my life," he replied, "I determined to get along with everybody. I noticed that all who became fine horsemen chose the most spirited horses. So I chose Xanthippe."

7 / An extraordinary evening

The civilization that reached its height in Athens in the fifth century B.C. was produced by a masculine society. The same was not true of all places in the Greek world; but at that time, as we have seen, the women in the families of Athenian citizens were kept closely at home. When an Athenian entertained his friends, his wife remained in the women's part of the house. There was no opportunity for romance among young members of Athenian families, though sometimes a deep love developed in marriage.

Romantic ardor, however, held an important place in Athenian life. Lads and very young men often possessed for a brief period a rare beauty which aroused admiration and sometimes led to devoted friendship. This was shown in various ways according to accepted traditions, frequently becoming the subject of good-natured teasing. Sometimes such ardor was valued as an incentive to courage and noble action. Homosexual relations, however, were not looked upon as perverted. Among those noted for physical beauty and personal charm were Charmides, Alcibiades, and the poet Agathon.

After winning the first prize for one of his tragedies, Agathon held a solemn sacrifice of thanksgiving to the gods for granting him victory, followed by a splendid banquet for friends and acquaintances. But the less formal dinner party at his house on the following night was more vividly remembered. On that occasion the speeches made by Socrates and Alcibiades were so surprising and so significant that for a long time they were repeated by men with good memories who had been present. An account of this evening is given in Plato's *Symposium*. To Athenians this word meant the period after a dinner in which diversion was provided for the guests while they drank their wine.

Socrates was met on his way to Agathon's by Aristodemus, an admirer whose devotion went so far as to make him adopt his teacher's habit of going barefoot. Surprised to see Socrates wearing sandals, he asked the reason.

"I'm going to Agathon's," Socrates replied. "I wasn't there last night, knowing how big a crowd he would have, but I promised to come today. Why not come with me?"

They walked on together, the young man feeling no more hesitation about going uninvited than Socrates had in asking him. But before they reached the house, Socrates was possessed by an idea on which he wanted to reflect.

"Go on," he said, "I'll follow soon."

All who knew Socrates were well aware of this habit. He would suddenly stand motionless for a while, completely absorbed in thought, and oblivious to anything outside himself.

Agathon's door stood open. A slave at once led Aristodemus into the dining-room, where most of the guests had already taken their places. As usual, they reclined on couches, before which slaves would soon put small individual tables. Socrates did not arrive until the meal was about half over, but a place had been saved for him next to Agathon.

After all had finished, they poured the customary libations to the gods and sang a hymn. But before the drinking began, one of the guests made an unusual proposal. Since he had not yet entirely recovered from having drunk too much on the preceding night, he suggested that instead of following the custom which compelled all to drain their cups to the last drop at the same time, each be allowed to drink as he felt inclined. This was strongly approved by Eryximachus, a doctor, who added, "I make an exception of Socrates. We all know that he is equally able to drink not at all or to drink as much as the most unrestrained."

Aristophanes, writer of comedies, laughed and said, "I certainly drowned myself last night."

"Since that pleases you," said Eryximachus, "I will make another suggestion. Let's send the flute-girl away to play to herself somewhere, or perhaps to the women of the household. Then we can entertain ourselves with speeches. I will even propose a subject. Phaedrus here has often complained to me that although countless poems have been written to praise other great divinities, one whom we would unite in calling very great indeed has been utterly neglected. Let each one of us now make a speech to honor the mighty god Love, starting with Phaedrus, then proceeding around in turn."

Those who afterward told their friends about the evening reported four speeches in addition to the startling two of Socrates and Alcibiades. The first three of these dealt with the love of an older man for an attractive youth.

Phaedrus began by declaring that Love was a great and wonderful god. He spurred a man toward honorable action, in order to win the admiration of one he loved, and kept him from doing anything cowardly or mean. Because of this, the god was a powerful influence for good.

Next in order was Pausanias, who although he had the same name as the writer of the ancient guidebook, lived some centuries earlier. He maintained that it was important to discriminate between two kinds of love; the common type, which was love of the body, and the exalted kind, which was love of the mind and soul.

When the latter was felt by both lover and beloved, both were constantly striving to become finer in every way.

The turn of Aristophanes came next; but having trouble with hiccups, he appealed to Eryximachus, the doctor, who was just beyond him.

"Either stop my hiccups, doctor," he demanded, "or speak in my place until they stop."

"I will do both," Eryximachus answered. "While I am speaking, try holding your breath for a time. If that doesn't help, gargle some water. If they still continue, tickle your nose with something until it makes you sneeze. After one or two sneezes you will have no more trouble."

Beginning his speech, the doctor accepted the distinction between common and exalted love, then developed the statement that such contrasts are to be noticed even in the field of medicine. The healthy parts of the human body have healthy desires, but any unhealthy part is likely to be afflicted with diseased cravings. The physician must know how to tell them apart and eliminate the latter, substituting for them desires that are beneficial. If he is a wise and skillful practitioner, he knows how to substitute the higher type of desire for the other.

When he concluded, Aristophanes was free from hiccups. "I tried each of your remedies, doctor," he said, "but it was the sneeze that cured me."

All settled themselves in delighted expectation of his speech, for they knew they were going to be amused.

Aristophanes proclaimed solemnly: "I shall begin by telling you about the earliest shape of human beings and how it came to be changed to what we see today.

"At first they were all perfectly round like spheres, each topped by one neck, with two faces placed back to back, and having four arms and four legs. Sometimes a man walked on two feet as we do, but when he wanted to get ahead very fast, he revolved like a wheel on all limbs with tremendous speed and power. This ability made men become so violent that the gods felt the only way to keep their own power would be to annihilate the human race.

"But when they realized that this would deprive them of all the sacrifices and gifts they had been enjoying, they hesitated. Then Zeus decided to cut each man in two, so making him weaker and at the same time doubling the number to make gifts to the gods. After cutting them as one might cut an apple, he had Apollo turn the one remaining face so it would look down upon the surface where the cut had been made and feel humbled.

"But each also felt incomplete, missing his other half and looking for it always. Some sought a female half, and some a male.

Whenever two halves that had been separated met again, they felt the utmost happiness and wanted to remain together.

"Therefore," said Aristophanes, "let us never again start to perform outrageous acts, as men did in their spherical shape, or Zeus may once more cut us in two, leaving us with only one eye and half a nose, as we hop on one foot."

All were laughing.

"So much has been said," the doctor commented, "that I should be afraid nothing could be added, if the two speakers that remain were any except Agathon and Socrates. But knowing both as I do, I am eager to listen."

"Think of the great difficulty," said Socrates, "in which I shall be left after Agathon has spoken."

"You're trying to put a spell on me, Socrates," said Agathon, "so that I will have stage fright at the thought of how much the audience is expecting of me."

"By no means," Socrates insisted. "I saw the poise with which you stood with the actors before the huge audience of citizens in the theater. Of course you would not be embarrassed to speak before so few as we are."

"Do you think," Agathon asked, "that I am so impressed by a theater filled with people that a few good judges are not more formidable to me than a crowd of undiscriminating men?"

"But we were part of the crowd then, and I am sure you did not invite your guests tonight because you had tested our qualifications as men of superior wisdom. Of course I know that if you had found someone truly wise, you would be ashamed to disgrace yourself before him, wouldn't you?"

"Yes."

"But you would not be ashamed before an ignorant crowd?"

Here Phaedrus interrupted. "Don't answer, Agathon. For if Socrates can get someone to question, he will forget everything else and go on asking questions all night. I enjoy nothing more than hearing him, but just now I must demand from each one his praise of the god Love."

"You are right," said Agathon, and began his speech.

He adopted the style of the sophist Gorgias, who aimed to impress his audience more by the sound of his words than by presenting a serious thought for their consideration. Among the characteristics of Gorgias that he imitated were frequent contrasts, rhyming words, and the piling up of either words or phrases.

Toward the end he said, "Love is fairest and rarest himself, and makes men fair and rare. By him none is harmed, but all are charmed. When he finds men together, he binds them together in festivals, in dances, and at sacrifices. He is sought by those who have not found him, and cherished by those who have. At time of toil or danger, in every wish or word, he is the best pilot, helper, defender, savior, the glory of gods and men, the fairest and noblest leader whom everyone should follow, joining in the song with which he delights divinities and magnifies mortals. My speech, Phaedrus," he concluded, "is half playful and half serious."

The listeners cheered.

Looking at the doctor, Socrates remarked, "Didn't I say that Agathon would speak in an amazing manner and place me in a difficult situation?"

"You did," said Eryximachus, "and the first part of your statement was correct. But that you are in any difficulty I do not believe."

"I will not make myself ridiculous by any attempt to rival Agathon," Socrates said, "but if you all want to hear the truth about love, spoken in words as they come to me, I am ready. Will you allow me to ask Agathon just a few questions as an introduction?"

After all had agreed, Socrates led Agathon to an admission that love is desire for what one wants, but does not yet have, and this desire is always for what is beautiful and good.

The speech that followed was long and serious, consisting entirely of what Socrates said he learned on several occasions from a wise and renowned priestess named Diotima. She had come to Athens many years before on a religious mission, and Socrates had reflected on her teaching ever since, making it a part of his thought and action. It may be that this experience caused him to believe that the ability of women was no less than that of men.

She surprised him first by declaring that, in spite of what many said, love was not a god, but a great spiritual power, intermediate between mortals and Divinity. "Through love," she claimed, "the prayers and sacrifices of men are conveyed to Divinity, for love spans the space that divides them, binding all together and carrying back to mortals commands and rewards from gods. The wisdom that understands this is spiritual, just as the wisdom that understands the various arts and crafts is practical."

At another time she said, "Love is the desire for the everlasting possession of the good and beautiful. At a certain age, human nature is moved by a desire to create in beauty. This is the mystery of man and woman, which is a divine thing, for conception and generation are a principle of immortality in a mortal creature. Men whose bodies only are creative seek women and beget children. But some have creative minds and souls. Among them are the poets and other artists who have the power of invention. These conceive and communicate wisdom, and they become the parents of excellence of every kind."

Diotima told Socrates that what she had mentioned were the lesser mysteries of love, which anyone might enjoy. Beyond them were the greater mysteries. She did not know whether Socrates would be able to rise to these, but she would try to indicate how he should proceed.

"One should begin when very young," she said, "and under a wise instructor, who would guide him to start by loving one beautiful form only. Out of that he should create beautiful thoughts. Soon he would himself perceive that the beauty of one form is related to the beauty of another. Then he would consider that his intense love of the one form was after all a small thing. So he would become a lover of all beautiful forms. This would lead to a realization that beauty of mind is something higher and more important than beauty of form. He would go on upward, from fine forms to fine minds and thoughts, then to fine actions, then fine conceptions. At last he would reach the idea of absolute beauty and know what it was. Then he would be able to create not merely images of beauty, but absolute beauty itself, free from any pollution."

"These, Phaedrus," said Socrates, "were the words of Diotima. I am convinced that what she told me is true. Now and always I shall honor love and urge others to do the same."

Just then they were startled by a vigorous pounding on the outer door and the shouts of a band of revelers. Agathon told the slaves to let them in, if they were friends.

They were led by Alcibiades, wearing a garland with many

ribbons attached. His face was glowing with enthusiasm as he proclaimed that he had come to crown Agathon for his victory in the theater. Taking the garland from his own head, he placed it on Agathon's.

"Sit here beside me," said Agathon. "There is room for three on this couch."

"Who is the other?" asked Alcibiades. Turning a little, he exclaimed, "I might have known. Socrates! I believe he lies in wait for me. I keep finding him in the most unexpected places. Here you are again, Socrates. And, as so often happens, beside the most handsome man in the whole room."

Socrates responded to his pretense of indignation. "Protect me, Agathon!" he appealed. "Ever since I became this man's admirer, he will not permit me to admire anyone else who has even the slightest claim to beauty. He may become violent now at any moment."

"Your punishment shall be postponed," said Alcibiades. "Instead, let me take some of the ribbons I gave you, Agathon, so I may crown the head of Socrates, who with his words is constantly winning victories over all men, not only in a theater like you!"

He did this to everyone's amusement, for the gay ribbons that suited the young laughing faces of Agathon and Alcibiades looked strangely out of place on Socrates. Then he continued, "Now I elect myself master of the drinking. Fill a large goblet," he directed the wine-pourer, "or no! fill the wine-cooler itself and hand it to me."

He poured all the contents of the large cooler down his own throat without pausing, then said, "Fill it again and give it to Socrates. Watch him now, all of you. It holds enough to make any man drunk, but it will have not the least effect on Socrates. He can drink any amount without showing a sign of having done so."

Calmly Socrates did what Alcibiades wanted.

"Do you mean we are to do nothing but drink?" the doctor asked in a complaining tone, "without any conversation at all?"

"That I leave to you. You prescribe, doctor. We will obey."

"Before you came, we agreed that each one should make a speech in praise of love, and all have just finished. But you have not spoken, yet you have drunk more than any except Socrates. Make a speech now, then impose a task on your neighbor."

"When Socrates is present, I positively will not praise anyone but him," Alcibiades asserted. "I'm afraid of what he might do to me."

"What are you planning, man?" asked Socrates. "To make them laugh at me?"

"I am going to speak the truth. Will you let me?"

"I will not merely let you. I urge you to speak the truth."

"That is exactly what I shall do. And you, Socrates, if at any moment I make a statement that is not entirely true, interrupt me at once and tell them so."

With a twinkle in his eye, he said, "I shall begin, friends, by saying that Socrates reminds me of something you may think ridiculous. But that is not my meaning, as I will soon explain. He makes me think of the funny figures of satyrs in the shops of the craftsmen."

Everyone laughed, for the plump figure of Socrates was indeed like the shape of these comical creatures.

"Their bodies are made to contain valuable articles," Alcibiades said, "for they are little boxes made to hold what is precious. People often use them to contain images of the gods. We have all seen that the masks of satyrs on the stage look definitely like Socrates. And he is like one particular satyr in another way. The satyr Marsyas is said to have first played the melodies from which are derived those that the gods sing on Olympus. These have a power possessed by no other music. For even when they are played by an ordinary flute-girl, they move the soul and reveal the longing of those who reach out to the gods for inspiration.

"But you, Socrates, possess the same influence by your words alone, without any music. When we hear the best of other speakers, this never happens. Your words, however, even when imperfectly repeated by another, amaze and possess the soul of anyone who hears them. They make my heart leap and tears spring to my eyes, and I have seen many others affected in the same way. No one else has ever made me ashamed or caused me to feel that I cannot bear to go on living in the way I do. I want to close my ears to all else and stay at the side of Socrates, growing old along with him. But as soon as I am away from him, I am overcome again by my love of popularity and sink back into my old habits.

"I believe that I know him better than anyone else, and I am going to prove this. You all know he is fond of handsome boys. So are the satyrs, but Socrates has a different reason. When I looked within at his serious purpose, what I saw was divine—beautiful and marvelous, making me feel I must do whatever he desired.

"I had a high opinion of my own charm, and at first I thought he was in love with me, as many others had already been. So the next time I took no attendant along.—Socrates, listen carefully, and if I say the least thing that is not true, declare it at once.—When we were alone together, I expected him to talk to me as others had, and I felt happy about it. But he talked exactly as he had done in public places, and when the sun set, I went home.

"At another time, I practiced wrestling with him, and again nothing happened. Therefore I decided I must use stronger methods. I invited him to dine alone with me.

"Listen, all of you, and excuse what I did then and what I say now. I led him on, talking about his usual subjects until it was too late for him to go home. Then I said the best thing for him to do was to sleep on the couch where he was, for we were still reclining where we had eaten, and the nights were warm.

"Then I said, 'I think that you are the only lover I have ever had who is truly worthy of me. Yet you seem to be too modest to speak. I am hoping that you will help me to become a better man. For this reason, I would not refuse any favor to you and I lay myself at your feet. Do what you think is best for us both.'

" 'It is late now,' he said. 'We will consider what is best another time.'

"Thinking I had succeeded, I went over to his couch, crept under the cover with him, and there I remained all night. But, as Socrates must admit, in the morning I rose as though I had remained at the side of my father or my elder brother.

"Imagine what I felt at being rejected! Yet I could not be angry or give up talking with him afterward whenever possible, so deeply did I feel compelled to admire his self-restraint, his high intelligence, and his innate courage.

"These qualities he also showed later when we were together in the army attacking Potidaea. There he not only surpassed me, but all the others in endurance and in ability to go without food. (Yet, when he was at a feast, he always seemed to be enjoying it more than anybody else.) It was the same with his ability to hold out against the cold. The winter was frightfully cold there in the north, and all others either stayed in or wrapped themselves up in everything they could get, covering their feet with felt and wool. But Socrates walked over the ice with feet still bare, and even so he managed to march better than the rest of us. In a battle where I was wounded, he saved my life. When the generals afterward were about to give me an award of honor, I said it should go to Socrates, but he insisted on my taking it.

"On a later occasion, when our army was retreating from Delium, I, being on horseback, was comparatively safe. Looking around, I saw that all others were running in every direction, but Socrates was walking calmly, exactly as he does in Athens, with his head held high, rolling his eyes—just as you have described him, Aristophanes. He was looking at friends and enemies alike, making it quite plain that anyone who attacked him would meet with strong resistance.

"One thing I forgot to mention about the way he talks. To those who listen to Socrates for the first time his words may seem ridiculous. But if they will look below the surface, they will find that his words have more meaning than any others they have ever heard, extending as they do to the whole duty of a good and noble man."

Some personal jesting followed. Then another band of revelers entered, and the fun became more uproarious. After many had left, and those remaining were all asleep except Socrates, Agathon, and Aristophanes, the three discussed the writing of tragedy and comedy, Socrates maintaining that, although it did not happen in Athens, it should be possible for the same genius to compose successfully in both forms.

Finally the other two became drowsy and fell asleep. Socrates then settled each more comfortably on his couch. He himself went home, for the sun was up. He passed the day exactly as usual.

8 / A walk in the country: the creative imagination at play

It was mid-morning when Socrates met Phaedrus in a street not far from the temple of Olympian Zeus. Unlike sophists, who preferred to have the stimulus of an audience, Socrates was equally ready to talk with one man alone.

Phaedrus was striding forward so purposefully that Socrates asked where he was going.

"To take a walk in the country outside the city wall. Since early dawn I've been at a house where the great orator Lysias is a guest."

"Now I know why you are so excited," said Socrates. "He has read you one of his speeches. In fact, I believe the scroll under your arm is a copy you brought away."

"Yes, and you shall hear it, if you have the time to listen."

"You know very well that nothing could keep me from listening to what Lysias wrote and Phaedrus admired. Let's turn off here and walk along the Ilissus till we find a good place to sit."

"Why not walk in the brook itself? Luckily I'm not wearing sandals today, but going barefoot like you. The water is delightfully clear, and it will keep our feet cool as the day grows hotter."

Before long, Phaedrus asked, "You see that tall plane-tree over there?"

"Yes."

"We shall rest in its shade close to the stream, and probably be cooled by a gentle breeze."

"Truly a delightful spot," Socrates said when they had reached it. The place had been marked as sacred by a simple shrine to Pan, the nature god, and the Nymphs. Offerings of country folk were near.

"The air," Socrates said, "is filled with lulling summer sounds and the delicate fragrance of the blossoms on that shrub. This gentle slope looks made to lie on," he added, stretching out, "and the grass is a perfect pillow."

Phaedrus meanwhile seated himself and began to unroll the scroll.

The speech was one of a kind popular at the time. In it the writer used all his ingenuity to support a false concept. His only purpose was to prove his cleverness by making untrue words sound convincing. Lysias pretended to address a boy whose devoted friendship he was trying to win. He admitted that he felt no love for his listener, but claimed that he deserved acceptance more than one who really loved.

Phaedrus read with obvious enjoyment, asking as soon as he finished, "What do you think of it, Socrates? Isn't the language the most dazzling you ever heard?"

"You did all you could to make it seem brilliant," Socrates replied. "You were in an absolute ecstasy. So much so that I almost caught the infection from you."

"Don't joke about it. Please answer me truly. What other Greek do you think ever made, or could make a better speech on the subject?"

"I can't name anybody off-hand, but I'm sure I've heard something better. In fact, I feel I myself could find something different and better to say."

"Never mind what you heard. Go ahead and make a different and better oration equally long on the same subject. If you do," he added, laughing, "I promise that I will set up golden statues, life-size, of both you and myself."

"You are a dear golden idiot, Phaedrus," Socrates replied, "if you think I can avoid all the arguments Lysias used. However, they will be presented in better order."

The enthusiasm of Phaedrus troubled Socrates, who felt he must somehow lead his young friend to understand the useless-ness of this kind of verbal display, and also the danger inherent in it. But he knew Phaedrus was still too much under the spell produced by Lysias to accept any definite criticism.

"I'll run through this speech very fast," said Socrates, "with my face covered. If I look at you, I'll be too ashamed to say such things."

The situation compelled him to argue in support of what he believed not to be true. He made it a little less difficult for him-self by saying that his speech would be that of a man who really loved the boy, but had pretended that he did not and argued that the boy should respond for that reason.

Suddenly he broke off, declaring, "That is enough."

Phaedrus objected. "I thought you were only half through. You have brilliantly shown why the real lover should be refused, but you haven't said a word yet about the reasons for accepting the non-lover. Do go on."

"I will simply add that the non-lover has the opposite qualities. Enough time has been wasted on both. I will cross the brook and go home."

"No, not yet, Socrates. The sun is directly overhead. It is the hottest part of the day. Let's stay until it begins to get cooler. We can talk over what has been said."

"Your enthusiasm for discussion, Phaedrus, is beyond every-thing," Socrates declared. "I believe there is no one in your generation (except Simmias*) who has caused so many speeches to be made, either by delivering them himself or forcing someone else to do so. Just this minute I am impelled to make another."

"Nothing could be better. But why?"

"As I was about to cross the brook, I felt the familiar sign that stops me when I am starting to do what I should not. I seemed

* On the last day of Socrates' life, Simmias had a final talk with him.

to hear a voice saying that it would not let me go until I had atoned for my sin against what is divine. Even while I was making the speech, I was troubled, feeling I might be sinning against the gods in order to receive honor from men. I must atone for the wrong I have been doing."

"What wrong?" Phaedrus was surprised.

"That was a dangerous speech you brought, and you led me to compose another just as dangerous."

"What do you mean?"

"In the first place, it was foolish. Besides, it was fundamentally impious. Could anything be worse?"

"No—if that is really true."

"Both speeches represented love as evil, which it is not. There was no truth in either of them. With a solemn manner, they pretended to mean something, in order to deceive the ignorant little men of earth and win fame among them. If anyone capable of true and fine feeling had heard them, he would have thought we had been brought up among the lowest type of human beings, and never seen any case of genuine love. I will retract that speech of mine by making one as true as it was false. I would advise Lysias to do the same. My recantation I shall make with head uncovered and no feeling of shame."

"Do this now, Socrates!" Phaedrus was very eager. "I promise to make Lysias retract his."

Since one reason given for accepting the non-lover was that he was completely sane, while the lover was not, Socrates first emphasized the fact that all so-called madness was not insanity. "Some of the greatest blessings a man can receive," he said, "come from a kind of heaven-sent madness granted to inspired prophets and poets. Therefore let no one frighten us by saying that a moderate lover is to be accepted instead of one possessed by madness of love. For we can prove that this madness is given to lover and beloved by divine power, to be the most uplifting experience with which they may be blest. I am well aware," he added, "that those who enjoy superficial cleverness would not agree with what I am about to say, but it will be believed by the truly wise."

With all his insistence on clear reasoning which could stand the test of examination, Socrates sometimes wanted to lead beyond its reach and resorted to his extraordinary power of imagination.

Passages revealing this, like the following, are among the most significant in the *Dialogues*. They are sometimes referred to as myths, because the Greek word *mythos* denoted tales of divinities and miraculous happenings in contrast to what was produced by logical reasoning.

"Any physical body that is moved only from without," he began, "has no soul, but one moved from within has a soul which causes the motion."

His imagination then pictured the soul as resembling a charioteer driving two horses, one representing good impulses and the other bad. "Both horses," he said, "are provided with wings, for the purpose of lifting the soul upward. When fully winged, the soul is raised even as far as the region where gods move and guide the universe. But when the soul loses its wings, it settles down on the earth and enters a mortal body. The wings are intended to raise it to the level where the immortal gods remain amid beauty, goodness, wisdom, and everything equally perfect by which the wings are nourished and made stronger. When wings do not receive this nourishment, they become gradually weaker, lose their feathers, and finally fall away.

"In the wide vault of heaven," Socrates continued, "Zeus rules, directing all other gods as they preside over their assigned activities. They pass to and fro in heaven, each accomplishing his own work, and anyone who wishes may follow, for rivalry does not exist there. Whenever a time of celebration comes around, Zeus in his chariot leads the way, and all follow him up to the highest part of heaven, passing beyond it into a region still higher. There they behold pure knowledge and absolute truth, more exalting than any poet on earth has ever described. Refreshed in spirit by this, they return to the interior of heaven.

"That is the life of gods," Socrates declared. "A mortal soul follows the divinity of his choice, and if he has succeeded in becoming enough like that divinity, he can just manage, as he stands in his chariot, to raise his head into the highest region and behold the ultimate wonders there. He is carried around in the revolution of the spheres, but has constant difficulty with his ignoble horse, which keeps pulling the chariot downward. Some mortal souls occasionally rise enough to get a glimpse of the glory, then are dragged down by the inferior horse, but many never succeed in beholding that radiance even for a moment. They long to see the lofty region, but are pulled down into a confusion of other plunging horses that tread upon one another, each trying to get ahead of, the rest. If the charioteers have not learned to control their horses, they are forced to return without ever having seen the higher region. They long to reach it because the food for the highest part of the soul is there and the wings also are nourished by this. There is a law of the goddess Adrasteia (Retribution) that the soul that attains any vision of absolute truth is kept from harm until the next period of spherical revolution, and the soul that always attains is always unharmed.

"The reason anyone is moved at sight of a beautiful person is because, even without clearly knowing it, he is reminded of the glimpse he had of absolute beauty, and he longs to experience the uplift it gave him during the revolution of the spheres. But if he has not learned to control his unruly horse, it will force him to rush upon the beautiful one, seeking physical satisfaction in one way or another, desiring to feel exaltation again, but failing to obtain it. Those, however, who have reverence as well as love for the beautiful, can develop a relation that confers the greatest blessing a mortal can receive. For them what the ignorant call the madness of love is truly a divine experience.

"Two persons who are drawn together by a lower degree of love become dear to each other and derive satisfaction, but it does not approach the experience of the two who share the highest type of love and together with mutual reverence devote themselves to philosophy. These move forward as close companions and in time their souls rise together in heavenly radiance on the same wings."

Thus Socrates, but with far more detail, made a speech to erase forever the memory of the one Phaedrus had compelled him to deliver before.

He concluded his recantation with an appeal. "This, dear god of love, is the best retraction it is in my power to make of my previous false speech. Forget it, I pray, and do not take from me my understanding of love that you yourself gave. If anything Phaedrus or I said in our former speeches displeased you, blame Lysias, for he is responsible. Tell him to turn his attention to the study of philosophy like his brother Polemarchus. Then he will no longer keep Phaedrus from devoting himself to discourses on both love and philosophy."

This reminded Phaedrus that a prominent politician had recently spoken with contempt of Lysias for being a speech-writer.

"But," Socrates objected, "it is no disgrace to write speeches. Disgrace would be involved in writing them badly."

Phaedrus, as he listened to the recantation of Socrates, had given up his idea that Lysias could compose a retraction of his speech. Now joy lighted his eyes as he said, "Let's have a discussion about good writing."

Socrates smiled. "I might have known you would want that," he said. "But we have time for it. The grasshoppers are talking their loudest in the midday heat, and I believe they are watching us. If they should see us gradually close our eyes and fall into a doze, they would think we were no better than sheep that sleep at noon. But if they see us continuing our talk, oblivious to their singing, like Odysseus when he sailed past the Sirens, then perhaps their delight might bestow on us the gifts they bring to men from the gods."

"Do they? I never heard that," said Phaedrus.

"Anyone loving music as you do should not be ignorant of it. The legend is that long ago these insects were men, but when the Muses were born, and created song, it enchanted them so they forgot everything else. They kept on singing, never pausing to eat or drink. After this caused their death, the Muses changed them into grasshoppers that sing all through their lives, and when they die, go straight to the Muses to tell each one what mortal honors her most. They tell Calliope and Urania which ones are devoting their time to philosophy. So we ought not to sleep through the hot hours of midday, but give that time to thoughtful talking."

"Yes, let's talk about good writing," said Phaedrus happily.

"We must first determine," Socrates suggested, "what we think are the rules for good speaking. Would you agree with me that the first rule is that the speaker should positively know in his own mind the truth of what he is going to say?"

Phaedrus liked this, but remarked that many claimed with much pride that rhetoric taught a man to lead his audience to believe what he said, whether it was true or not. That was one reason for their practicing with such subjects as Lysias had chosen.

It took some time, but Socrates finally succeeded in bringing

Phaedrus to see that no one could become truly a master of the art of speaking unless he knew the truth about his subject.

"Now," said Socrates, "let us consider how Lysias constructed his speech."

Beginning to unroll the scroll, he commented at once, "He began with what should be at the end. Then followed, as you see, a confused mass of statements, each introduced because it happened to come into his head, without being developed from what preceded. It is better to begin with a general definition of one's subject, and follow with arguments arranged in an orderly way with reference to each other and to the whole. At the end, there should be a summing up of the arguments."

After fully considering the art of speaking, Socrates added, "To be a good speaker, a man should know the truth about his subject. But that is not enough. He must also understand his audience, the mental capacity of most of its members and their differing points of view. With all this in mind, he must make every effort to say—not what they may want to hear, but what would please any god who happened to listen, for gods have greater knowledge than any man."

Socrates would not let their discussion end without some consideration of written speeches. He began with a myth.

"I have heard a tradition," he said, "that in early times in Egypt, when Thamus was king, the god Theuth, whom Greeks call Ammon, came to him to teach things for him to pass on to his subjects, such as mathematics. After a time, he taught the alphabet, so that men could learn to write.

" 'This,' he said, 'will make the Egyptians wiser and improve their memories. It is a recipe for memory and wisdom!'

"But the king looked sad.

" 'Most ingenious god,' he answered, 'he who invents is not always the best judge of his invention and its usefulness. You have created not a recipe for remembering, but only a convenient reminder. It will implant in the minds of men not memory, but forgetfulness. Knowing they possess it in writing, they will no longer train their memories, but turn more and more often to written records.' "

Phaedrus smiled and said with a mischievous expression, "It is easy for you, Socrates, to make up myths and attribute them to others."

"What matters, Phaedrus," said Socrates seriously, "is not who first said something, but whether it is true. That is always for you to consider and decide."

"I deserved the reproof," Phaedrus admitted, "and I believe King Thamus was right."

The written word, Socrates believed, was an unsatisfactory substitute for the presence of the writer himself. A reader might misunderstand or get only an incomplete idea of what the writer meant. If the two were face to face, the writer could explain and answer questions until he was convinced that the impression on the other's mind was correct and complete.

"Best of all," Socrates said to Phaedrus, "is when one who has acquired true knowledge finds a congenial soul and, by use of dialectic, plants in his mind words that grow there and produce other seeds to become fruitful in other minds. So may continue the creation of new plants and seeds of everlasting truth. That is the kind of man, Phaedrus, whom you and I would pray to become."

"That, Socrates, is my earnest desire."

"Go now and tell Lysias that we went to the stream—and school—of the Nymphs and they told us to give this message to him. If his speeches are based on knowledge of truth, and he can defend them by arguments even stronger, he is worthy of a higher name than orator."

"What is that, Socrates?"

"Wise I may not call him, for wisdom belongs only to God. Lysias will be then a lover of wisdom or philosopher."

"I will tell him that, Socrates. The breeze is growing cooler now, isn't it? Shall we go?"

"Should we not first offer a prayer to the divinities by whose shrine we have been learning?"

Phaedrus agreed. Then Socrates prayed:

"Dear Pan, and all you other divinities who are here, grant that I may become beautiful within. May all that I do or say be in accord with my inner self. Let me understand that real wealth is the possession of the wise man only. Of gold, let me have merely so much as a moderate man needs.—Should we ask for anything more, Phaedrus?"

"Nothing more. Let this be my prayer as well."

9 / The courage
of his convictions

The exact time when Socrates discussed rhetoric with the famous sophist, Gorgias, is not known. The dialogue in which Plato presents this reveals Socrates anticipating the accusation before an Athenian court, which in 399 B.C. did sentence him to death. Whether this talk took place shortly before the trial, or some time earlier, Plato did not consider important, or he would have indicated the fact.

What should be understood is Socrates' knowledge that his method of conducting the great effort of his life might have this result. Understanding of the risk did not arouse in him the slightest doubt that he was doing right. Once he had resolved to lead his fellow Athenians to understand that they were being misled by clever, unethical speakers, whom they admired and imitated, he never faltered.

Gorgias showed respect for Socrates, as Protagoras also had, but similarly was not convinced, though he was willing to answer in a passage of dialectic. Early in their talk he stated that rhetoric was one of the arts which produced all of its effects through the use of words.

"To what class of things," Socrates asked, "do the words relate?"

"The greatest and best of human things," Gorgias answered. "They give freedom to men, and for rulers they supply the power to rule. Rhetoric enables men to persuade judges in the courts, senators in the council, citizens in the assembly, people at any public meeting."

Socrates then brought up the difference between belief and knowledge. This difference, they agreed, was that there could be a false belief as well as a true one, but that knowledge existed only with truth.

Gorgias referred to occasions when he had helped his brother, a doctor. Sometimes a patient refused to accept the medicine or the surgery that the doctor knew was the only thing that would cure. He then called Gorgias to persuade the patient to accept the treatment, and Gorgias, aided by rhetoric, often succeeded. But Gorgias admitted that what rhetoric did was to implant in a listener's mind belief, which might be false. When this happened, it resulted from a bad use of rhetoric, for which the speaker should be blamed, not his teacher.

Suddenly Polus intervened, and the dialogue became one between him and Socrates. He was a young sophist, an enthusiastic pupil of Gorgias, angry because Gorgias was not able to refute Socrates, and entirely without his master's courtesy.

"Socrates," he said, "do you actually believe what you are implying? Do you think anyone will believe that Gorgias does not know how to teach justice? That is unpardonably rude."

"My dear Polus," said Socrates with a friendly smile, "we Athenians acquire friends as well as children, so that when we grow old and stumble, they who are young may set us straight again both in action and in speech. If Gorgias and I are stumbling in our discussion, you are here to set us right. I am willing to retract any mistake I may have made—so long as you do not insist on making a long speech, but will ask and answer questions briefly."

"What?" demanded Polus indignantly. "Am I not to be allowed to say as much as I please?"

"It would indeed be shocking, my friend, were you to be deprived of that privilege on coming to Athens, where there is more freedom of speech than in any other city of the Greek world. If you have any desire to set me right, take back anything you wish from what has been said, then ask and answer as Gorgias and I have been doing."

"Very well, I will ask, Socrates. What is rhetoric?"

"Do you mean what kind of art?"

"Yes."

"Not an art at all, Polus, if I am to tell you the truth."

"Then what is it?"

"A means to create a certain delight and gratification."

"If it creates gratification," Polus demanded triumphantly, "must it not be a fine thing?"

"Why ask me that before I have completely defined it? As you think so much of gratifying people," Socrates said with a smile, "will you gratify me in one small way?"

"I will."

"Will you ask me what sort of art cookery is?"

"Of course. What sort of art is cookery?"

"Not an art at all."

"Then what is it?"

"A means of creating a kind of delight and gratification."

"Then are cookery and rhetoric the same?"

"By no means," replied Socrates. "They are different parts of the same process."

"What is that?"

"I am afraid," said Socrates, "that if I say what I truly think, it may seem discourteous to Gorgias. I do not want him to imagine I am ridiculing his profession. Whether what I have in mind is the art of rhetoric that Gorgias says he practices, I really do not know. The rhetoric I mean is a part of what is not one of the truly fine things."

"Of what is it a part, then, Socrates? Tell me this without any hesitation."

"To me," replied Socrates, "it appears to be not an art, but a process created by a bold and skillful mind that planned to make an impression on an audience. This process I call a kind of flattery, which has many forms, of which rhetoric is only one."

Polus demanded quickly, "What part is rhetoric?"

"According to my view, the shadow of a part of politics."

Without an instant's pause, Polus demanded, "Noble or ignoble?"

"Ignoble, I believe, if I am compelled to answer. But I doubt if you fully understand what I have been saying."

"By Zeus, Socrates, I certainly don't," said Polus.

Gorgias added, "Indeed, Socrates, I cannot say that I understand either."

"Naturally, Gorgias," said Socrates, "for I have not yet explained. But Polus is a spirited young colt, and quickly runs away." (This is a pun in Greek, for the young man's name is a word for colt.)

"Never mind him, but explain it to me," said Gorgias.

The explanation was long, but led to a statement that to Socrates it appeared that a cook aimed only to please the sense of taste, and therefore might serve what was even bad for the health of those he fed. Similarly, the rhetorician might advise lawmakers in a way that would accomplish his own aim, even though it was unjust.

Polus then returned to his part in the argument with Socrates. He had been fascinated by rhetoric and dazzled by superficial success. A significant moment in their talk came when Socrates said that injustice was the greatest of evils.

"Is that really true?" Polus asked. "Isn't suffering injustice a much greater evil than being unjust?"

Socrates replied, "No, indeed."

"Do you actually mean, Socrates, that you would choose to be wronged by someone, rather than to do wrong?"

"I would not choose either, Polus. But if one or the other absolutely must be, I would rather be wronged."

It took Socrates some time to lead Polus to an admission that the man who consciously committed an injustice was by that act implanting evil in his own character. The next step should be to have it removed. This could be done by punishment, and the guilty person should not only accept, but desire punishment. So the evil in him would be uprooted, and not remain to become malignant, poisoning the whole and finally becoming incurable.

"That sounds very strange to me," said Polus, "but perhaps it is the logical conclusion from your premise."

Callicles, in whose house they had met, intervened, and the dialogue shifted to him and Socrates. He was sitting beside Chairephon and suddenly whispered to him, "Is Socrates serious, or only joking?"

"I believe he is perfectly serious," Chairephon answered. "Why don't you ask him?"

"By the gods," exclaimed Callicles, "I will! Tell me, Socrates, are you serious or joking? If you are serious, and if what you say is true, wouldn't that mean that we men have turned life upside down and are doing the very opposite of what we should?"

"If any two individuals, Callicles, did not have some feelings that were alike, it would be utterly impossible for them to communicate with each other. Both you and I love our close personal friends, but each of us also loves something larger. You love the Athenian majority whose vote prevails in the assembly. Whenever the majority changes, you change. But I love philosophy, and that does not change. What philosophy has taught me, I will continue to believe, unless it can be refuted by logical proof. Philosophy has taught me that to do injustice and escape punishment is the worst of evils."

"You carry it too far," Callicles returned. "That is what is wrong with you, Socrates. Philosophy is well enough, if one partakes of it in moderation during early youth; but if followed too far, it can ruin a man's life, robbing him of many pleasures that naturally belong to mankind. These he could have, if he made himself stronger and more powerful than others. As a part of education, philosophy is excellent, but if one follows it too long, one will miss all that brings success in political life.

"I like you, Socrates," Callicles continued, "that is why I am telling you this. You are being careless, when you ought to be careful. Your nature is truly noble, but you do not know the rhetorical way to prove it in the manner that convinces an audience today. If you should ever be brought into court and accused falsely, the malicious accuser would win his case, even if he demanded the penalty of death for you. You seem to me, Socrates, to be confident that you will never be accused by some spiteful person."

Socrates answered, "I should indeed be utterly without intelligence, Callicles, if I did not realize that in this city today any man may have that experience. But this I positively know: if I am brought into court on such a charge, my accuser will be an ignoble person, for no worthy man would accuse one who had done no wrong. It would not be surprising, however, if I should be condemned to death. Shall I tell you why I expect this?"

"By all means."

"I believe that I am one of a very few Athenians—perhaps the only one—who practices the true art of politics. Whenever I speak, I do not try to please the listeners, but to tell what is truly best for them. If I am brought to trial, it will be as if a physician were being tried before a jury of little boys, on the indictment of a cook. The accuser would say, 'This man, boys, has done many bad things to you. He cuts you and burns you. He makes you swallow bitter drinks, he compels you to go hungry and thirsty. How different from the fine meats and desserts I prepared for you!'

"What could the doctor say in his defense? Only 'All this I did in order to make you healthy.' And how loud that jury of boys would cry out against him!"

"They probably would."

"That is what would happen to me. If anyone declares that I corrupt young men or criticize those who are older, I will be able to reply only that I do this to make justice clear and thus to benefit all citizens. Therefore I may suffer anything."

"Do you think a man so defenseless in his city is in a good position?"

"Yes, Callicles, if he has never said or done anything wrong in his relations with men or toward the gods. To make this clear, I should like to tell you a myth, if you do not object."

"Then tell it."

"You may think it merely fanciful, but I believe it contains a truth. Homer tells us that Zeus dethroned the god who had previously ruled, but had been unjust. Then he divided the domain, keeping the sky for himself, giving the sea to his brother Poseidon, and to his other brother, Pluto, all that was below the surface of the earth, including the world of the dead. According to a law regarding the destiny of man, anyone who had lived justly all his life was sent to the islands of the Blest, to dwell in perfect happiness, but those who had lived unjustly were sent to the place of punishment.

"For some time the judgment was given just before death. The judges were alive and the men still alive. But when it was evident that some of the judgments were not well given, Pluto and the authorities from the islands of the Blest came to Zeus to complain that some souls were being sent to the wrong places. Zeus replied, 'I shall make this impossible. The trouble is that judges and men are alive, and of course wearing clothes. Hereafter, men shall be judged after death by immortal judges. Many men whose souls are filled with injustice by evil acts wear fine garments and bring to court witnesses who swear that they have lived righteously and so succeed in impressing the judges. From now on, the naked soul of the man shall face the naked soul of his judge.'

"It is my belief, Callicles," Socrates continued, "that death is the separation of a man's soul from his body. The body remains at first as it was the moment before death. Similarly, the soul remains at first what the man's life has made it. I infer that his habits have left their marks to some extent and for a time. The lies he has told and the evils he has committed have left ugly scars and open wounds.

"You may think this is all foolishness, and turn from it in scorn. And there would be reason for doing so, if we could find something better and more true. But that has not happened. I shall continue to do all I can to present my soul undefiled when it is finally to be judged. I shall seek always to know the truth, to live as well as I can, and when the time comes to die, to die as well as I can. And I exhort all other men, to the utmost extent of my power, to join me in this effort. Nothing in life is greater or more important."

10 / Politics, prejudices and the accusation

The accusation and trial of Socrates which led to his death in 399 B.C. proceeded according to Athenian law. For that reason he never protested against the result.

He believed, however, that he did not deserve condemnation. This he made clear in his speech at the trial. In the writings of Plato it is called the *Apology,* a misleading title to the English-speaking person. The Greek word *apologia* was the technical term for a defendant's speech. It was the opposite of an apology, as we commonly use the word. In it the accused man defended his conduct. In this case he obviously aggravated the passions of the majority of the 501 Athenians constituting the jury.

Socrates realized he was doing this, but it was the culmination of the great effort of his life. Among the jurors were undoubtedly some who had never listened to him. If he could make even a few of them understand what he had been trying to do, his trial would have accomplished something, whatever might be the verdict.

To gain any comprehension of what happened, it is necessary to know about the confused, but intensely passionate, emotions and prejudices which dominated Athenians at the time.

When the Peloponnesian War ended with the complete victory of Sparta in 404 B.C., the conquerors brought about the establishment of a body of thirty Athenians to draw up new laws, and to manage public affairs until the code was completed. These were men who had opposed the Athenian democracy. Many had been exiles, but returned after Athens was defeated, for Sparta never favored democratic governments.

The Thirty Tyrants, as they came to be called, ruled in Athens from September in 404 to May in 403 B.C. Most of them used their power to further their individual aims and satisfy personal enmities. They proclaimed an intention to purge the city of wrong-doers, and under this excuse arrested citizens and condemned them to death, especially if they possessed wealth the tyrants were determined to confiscate. It was a period of frightening uncertainty. No one could expect justice, and every kind of personal hostility was a constant threat.

Most prominent among the Thirty was Critias, a former exile who belonged to a distinguished family. He had been a pupil of Gorgias and a friend of Socrates, and had himself won a reputation as an orator, a poet and a philosopher. Only his political views seem to have been held against him before he became one of the Thirty, but in that position he committed outrageous acts.

The crimes of the Thirty led many democrats to leave Athens. Two of them, Thrasybulus and Anytus, with a few followers, seized an Athenian fortress near the northern frontier, and the army the Tyrants sent to blockade it was driven back by a snowstorm. After a time, Thrasybulus gathered additions to his small army and seized the port Piraeus. A battle was fought nearby in which Critias was killed. Then it was not long before the rest of the Thirty were deposed, after which a Spartan general, named Pausanias, came to Athens to help establish order. He worked with Thrasybulus and the result was a reconciliation of the opposing parties of Athenians. The terms were a general and mutual pardon for all except the Thirty and those involved in carrying out their commands. Until a new democratic constitution could be formed, the earlier democratic laws were to be enforced.

But while former opponents were gradually adjusting themselves to reconciliation, many continued to be swayed emotionally by their strong personal prejudices. Conspicuous among these was Anytus, who, because of his participation with Thrasybulus in overthrowing the Thirty, had great influence.

His violent dislike of all sophists is vividly shown in a short passage of Plato's dialogue *Meno*. When we consider that many persons had been classing Socrates with the sophists, because they did not know him well enough to understand him, we can get a better comprehension of what happened in 399 B.C.

Meno and Socrates were talking in a public place, when the former asked, "Can you tell me whether a man becomes truly good by being taught, or by practice of some kind, or simply by nature, or perhaps even in some other way?"

This gave Socrates the kind of opportunity he liked. He said he did not know exactly what goodness was, nor had he ever found anyone who did.

Meno at once declared it was easy to define. Goodness was ability to command in affairs of state, of course helping friends and harming enemies and taking care that no one harmed him. Obviously there was no thought behind this definition. Socrates replied that tyrants have power to command, but they often do this unjustly, and no unjust person is truly good. The same kind of rebuttal deflated Meno, when, far from being a serious thinker, he offered other definitions.

Suddenly Socrates said, "Look, Meno! Anytus has just seated himself not far away. Let's ask him about this. He should be able to help us. His father was highly intelligent and became wealthy through his own good sense and industry. The Athenians have confidence in Anytus, for they have elected him to the highest positions."

He called out, "Anytus, do help your friend here. He wants to learn how to be both wise and good, so as to be able to take part in managing affairs of state. Oughtn't he to go to the men whose profession is to teach exactly this, and who declare that they are ready to instruct anyone who wants to learn? For years they have been well paid for practicing this profession."

"Whom do you mean, Socrates?"

"You must know, Anytus. People call them sophists."

"Stop, Socrates! Don't say another word to me about them. I certainly hope that no relative or friend of mine—no, nor any citizen or even visiting stranger, will ever become so utterly mad as to go to a sophist. They corrupt and destroy everybody they get hold of."

"That is a strange thing to say, Anytus," Socrates remarked. "There was Protagoras, I remember, who had taught forty years before he died, and earned more by his teaching than Phidias, the greatest of sculptors. Do you think Protagoras was corrupting his disciples for all those years without being detected? The whole Greek world admired him, and his high reputation has continued since his death. Can men thought the wisest of teachers by so many people have been out of their minds?"

"Far from it, Socrates. Those who were out of their minds were the young men who gave money to them. So were the relatives and guardians who did not prevent this—and most wrong were the cities that allowed sophists to come in. All of them should have been driven out, whether citizens or strangers."

"Has one of the sophists injured you, Anytus? Is that why you are so bitter against them?"

"Of course not. I never had anything to do with a sophist, nor would I allow any of my family to consult one."

"You are entirely unacquainted with them?"

"And may I always remain so!"

"Then, Anytus, how can you know whether their teaching is good or bad, if you have never known even one?"

"I know quite well what kind of men they are. That's enough."

"To whom, then, would you advise Meno to go in order to learn how to become eminent in political life? That is what he wants to know, and he is a friend of your family."

"Why don't you advise him?"

"I told him that men had established themselves as teachers of this, but you think I made a bad mistake. Perhaps I did. For that reason I wish you would tell him."

"Why name an individual?" Anytus asked. "An Athenian of the upper class, if Meno will follow his instruction, will do him more good than all the sophists."

"Did they develop this knowledge by themselves without learning from anyone?"

"I suppose," Anytus answered, "that they learned it from the preceding generation. There have been many fine men in Athens."

"True. But were they able to teach their goodness to others? The sons of superior statesmen often prove inferior to their fathers."

While Socrates elaborated by giving examples, Anytus listened, becoming more and more irritated. Suddenly he rose, his eyes blazing.

"Socrates," he exclaimed, "you slander too many men! I advise you to take care. In most cities, and in Athens particularly, it is easier to do harm than good. You must know that." He rushed angrily away.

Socrates said quietly, "Anytus is in a rage. It does not surprise me. He thinks I believe him inferior to his father. But when he comes to understand that is not the case, and truly realizes what I am trying to discover, he will feel differently toward me."

Perhaps Socrates was remembering how the blind rage of Thrasymachus had melted away. But Thrasymachus had listened long enough to understand that Socrates was entirely free from personal hostility; and that his one desire, untainted by any lower motive, was to discover what was true. Unfortunately Anytus never had this experience. He remained one of the not inconsiderable number of Athenians who thought Socrates was like the sophists, except that, for some obscure reason, he did not demand payment—one of several ways in which they felt him to be queer.

The average Athenian, and many other Greeks as well, had a strong prejudice against men he thought too clever. The use of intelligence to deceive appears in their literature as early as Homer's *Odyssey* and as late as the *Medea* of Euripides. Anytus shared the prejudice, and also the resentment of the average Athenian if his prejudices were questioned.

Not long after his encounter with Anytus, Socrates received official information that he must present himself for trial on a charge of impiety, brought against him by someone named Meletus. This proved to be a little-known young man, and many assumed that he had been prompted by Anytus.

The actual charge was: "Socrates is guilty of corrupting the young men of Athens and of not believing in gods that this city accepts, but in other new divinities."

The first part of the charge was what Anytus believed about sophists, and probably about Socrates as well. The latter part seems to have been a misconception of rumors about his "familiar sign."

Soon after Socrates was informed that he would be brought to trial on a charge of impiety, he happened to meet Euthyphro, a respected soothsayer and authority on religious duties. Welcoming the opportunity, Socrates questioned him as to the nature of piety and impiety. He then gave three different definitions, but not one stood the test of reasoning. In the course of their talk, Euthyphro referred to the familiar myth about how Zeus dethroned his father.

Socrates asked at once, "Do you believe those stories? That the gods quarreled and fought one another? I cannot. That divine beings should be guilty of such actions I am unable to accept, even though artists have represented them in statues and paintings."

In this statement of his own belief, Socrates was revealing an ethical standard higher than that of his companion. But he was also demonstrating his inability, even when his life might depend upon the influence of just such Athenians as this one, to suppress his quest for truth.

11 / *In court*

No official records of speeches were made in ancient Greece, but two works entitled *Defense of Socrates* have survived, one by Plato, the other attributed to Xenophon. In the former, Plato is mentioned as present, and is generally believed to have written it not long after. Xenophon had left Athens more than a year before and was still in Asia on a military expedition. No one thinks that Plato reproduced the exact words of Socrates, but as they had been closely associated for ten years, we may be justified in believing that he would not have put in the mouth of the teacher he revered anything that was not part of the man's thought. The account that follows is based on this.

Through approximately the first half of the defense, the tone appears surprisingly light, but the remainder is absolutely serious. In some *Dialogues* also, a similar combination may be observed. The union of courage and humor at times in Plato's *Apology* may remind one of that moment in Shakespeare's *Romeo and Juliet* when Mercutio, knowing that he has received a fatal wound, says of it, " 'Tis not so deep as a well, nor so wide as a church door—but 'tis enough, 'twill serve."

Socrates began with a statement that, though he was past seventy, he had never before been required to appear in an Athenian court. This lack of experience, he claimed, entitled him to ask the jury not to be watching for rhetorical effects, as they often were, but to consider only what was true and just.

The first point Socrates emphasized was that for many years people in Athens who did not understand his aim, but were annoyed by the interest he aroused in young men, had been circulating false reports about him. He could not give their names because these incorrect statements were not made when he was present, so he had no chance to refute them. He knew, however, that they were widely accepted and repeated, as derogatory remarks frequently are. Socrates declared that if the jury should convict him, it would be a result of prejudice based on ignorance and misunderstanding.

Taking up the charge of Meletus, after mentioning that it was prompted by Anytus, Socrates took advantage of a regular custom in trials at the time. A defendant could, if he wished, ask questions of his accuser, who must answer them. By his answers Meletus showed his inability to support the accusation he had been told to bring into court.

"Tell me, Meletus," Socrates said, "do you consider it important that our young men should become morally excellent?"

"I certainly do," Meletus answered with obvious confidence.

"Then tell the jury, if you please, who makes them so. You must be sure of this, since you have made it your concern to discover who corrupts them and have brought me to trial on that charge."

Meletus remained silent.

"Don't you see, Meletus, that your silence proves you have not been thinking deeply about the matter? Please answer the question. Who makes our young men better?"

"The laws." Meletus thought this would be a safe reply.

"I did not ask *what*, but *who*—what person?"

"These men, Socrates. The jurors." Meletus remembered that it was considered a good plan to flatter an Athenian jury.

"Do you mean, Meletus, that these jurors are able to instruct young men and make them improve?"

"Of course I do."

"All of them?" There were 501.

"Absolutely all," he said confidently.

"What about the listeners here in court? Do they make the young men better?"

"Yes."

"And the members of the council?"

"Yes."

"And the members of the assembly?"

"They also."

"How marvelously fortunate our young men are!" Socrates exclaimed. "All of the Athenians are making them better but me. I am the only one who corrupts them. Is that what you say?"

"Yes, indeed. I say that most emphatically." Even this absurdity could not make Meletus alter the charge he had been instructed to bring.

Socrates asked more questions, causing Meletus to appear increasingly ridiculous. Then he said to the jury: "Many people in the city hold a strong prejudice against me. This is what will convict me, if I am convicted. Not Meletus or Anytus, but the slander and resentment of ignorant people. These things have convicted many good men in the past, and will undoubtedly do so in the future. It is not strange that this should happen to me."

Many on the jury were probably among those prejudiced against him because Critias and Alcibiades in their early years had been his friends. Both were already dead, but the harm they had done was far from forgotten. Critias had been the most criminal of the Thirty Tyrants, and Alcibiades had left Athens during the Peloponnesian war and gone to help her greatest enemy, Sparta. These facts were undoubtedly in the minds of many jurors, for Athenians who did not understand Socrates believed those two were examples of his bad influence on young men. Plato, however, never implied that Socrates had any lasting

effect on either.

From this point on, the speech of Socrates was profoundly serious. "All citizens of Athens," he said, "have served in her army, where we obeyed the commander without allowing ourselves to consider our own safety.

"We must remember that we live in a city renowned for wisdom and strength. Therefore we should not be concerned about winning fame or political honors. We should try rather to gain more intelligence, to arrive at more knowledge of truth, and to develop finer character. This is what I advise and urge, whether I am talking to a young man or an old one, whether to a citizen or a foreigner, for it is the command of Divinity to mortal men.

"This is the only thing I teach. Whether you do what Anytus wishes or not, whether you release or convict me, I will continue to urge everyone to do this, even if you could put me to death over and over again.

"It is for your sakes I am making this defense, not for my own. If you sentence me to death, you will do far more harm to yourselves than to me."

Socrates then compared the city to a large horse of fine breed that had grown lazy and needed to be roused to its proper activity by a stinging gadfly. It is annoying, he said, to be roused when starting to fall asleep, and the natural impulse is to strike and kill the insect that stings, or at least drive it away. Socrates believed he had been granted insight into the minds of many Athenians in order that he might awaken them to realize the mental and ethical sluggishness into which they were sinking. It would pull them down, he feared, from the height to which they had risen in the last hundred years. What he really deserved, he said, was to be awarded the honor bestowed on public benefactors.

To prove that fear of being put to death would never force him to commit an unjust act, he told about two occasions in his life—first while the city was still a democracy, and later under the rule of the Thirty Tyrants.

A most disgraceful act committed by the Athenian assembly of citizens—one of which they were afterward bitterly ashamed—occurred in 406 B.C. after a naval battle off the coast of Asia Minor. By a strange irony of chance, Socrates, who constantly avoided taking part in political life, found himself for one disastrous day a member of the group presiding in the assembly. To his horrified amazement, the people, in a frenzy of grief and anger, insisted on an illegal motion. The law of Athens required that no one should be put to death without having been tried alone in court and condemned. But in spite of this, they executed in a group, and without any trial, all the commanders of the expedition, because they had come away from the battle without first recovering the bodies of the dead, as their religious and military duty required. Socrates alone cast his vote against it. Though some at once threatened to kill him if he would not join in carrying out their will, he remained firm.

The other incident was one of a kind frequent under the Thirty Tyrants, but the action of Socrates was startlingly different from that expected. The Thirty often ordered a few citizens to come to their office, and commanded them to bring for trial a man the tyrants wanted to condemn so that they could appropriate his wealth. Socrates was summoned with four others and told to go across to the island of Salamis and arrest a certain Leon. On leaving the office, the other four carried out the order, but Socrates was seen calmly walking through the crowded city to his own home. His friends believed the Thirty would have had him killed for this, if they had not been deposed almost immediately after.

"You may ask," Socrates said, "why so many people want to pass so much time with me. They enjoy hearing me question those who think they have much wisdom, but really lack it. This can be amusing. But I ask these questions with the hope of leading men to understand their need of true wisdom and to begin seeking for it. If this corrupts young men, those who have grown older and realized the fact should all have come forward long ago and accused me. Or if they did not, their relatives should have done so. I see here in court many who have listened to me—Crito, for instance, whose age is the same as mine, and his son, Critobulus."

After calling attention to many others, among them Adeimantus and Plato, Socrates continued, "If I corrupted these, why didn't Meletus call upon them and their relatives? If he never thought of it, let him call them forward now. I will grant him the time. But the fact is that they are all ready to support me, because they know I am speaking the truth."

In conclusion he said: "Men of Athens, I do believe in divine power in a higher sense than my accusers do, and I am ready to accept the decision of God as to what result of this trial will be best both for me and for you."

Socrates often referred to "the gods," like other Greeks. But occasionally, when most serious, he used a singular instead of a plural form. It seems best to suggest their rare solemnity by using "God" in English. Either "the god" or "a god" would mean only one of "the gods."

The required majority of the 501 jurors voted him "Guilty." Socrates said this did not surprise him so much as the fact that if only thirty of them had voted the opposite way, he would have been acquitted.

Impiety was considered a crime, but the penalty for it was not established by law. In such cases, it was customary for the accuser to propose the penalty he wanted, and for this to be followed by the defendant's offer of a different penalty. Then the jury voted for its choice between the two.

Meletus demanded death. The general expectation was that Socrates would propose exile. That would take him out of Athens, which was what Anytus and some others wanted. But exile was an evil. Socrates would not propose an evil, because it would indicate he agreed that he had done wrong and deserved punishment. In his last words to the jury he emphasized what he had previously said about having been a benefactor of Athens. More of the jury than had voted him guilty chose the death penalty.

There was a delay before Socrates was led to prison. Plato indicated that his unhappy friends, some of them in the jury's minority, gathered about Socrates, and he spoke to the entire group.

The Greek language enabled him to make a subtle, but devastating, distinction. Throughout his defense he had addressed the jurors as "men of Athens." This expression would have been used by anyone speaking before people gathered in a public place. The term regularly used in trials, when given its full significance, meant "men who administer justice." Not once had Socrates used this, and his avoiding it undoubtedly irritated many. Socrates used it now when speaking directly to the minority who had voted for acquittal. "I call you that who voted

to acquit me," he said, "because that is what you really are."
There could be no more powerful way of indicating that their
vote was just and the vote of the majority had been unjust,
though legally cast.

He then made it clear that he did not think the decision of the
jury was the result of any mistake made by him in defending
himself, because not at any time had his familiar sign indicated
to him that he should check himself in what he was saying.
Therefore he believed that death could not be a bad thing.

Understanding the deep misery of his listeners, he went on to
say that death was one of two things—either complete un-
consciousness or, as some believed, a departure of the soul (the
real person) from the body to another region. If the former was
true, everyone knew that a night undisturbed by dreams or
wakefulness was better than any other. If it was true that the
soul entered a different region,—here Socrates indulged his
imagination and his recurrent sense of humor.

"If that is true," he suggested, "then one could meet those who
indeed administer justice, instead of merely pretending to, and
meet also the souls of many who had been unjustly condemned.
Think how interesting it would be to compare experiences with
them! and how interesting to question them, as I had done in
life, to find out which among them had true knowledge, and
which only thought they had. No one there would be condemned
to death for dong this, since all would be immortal."

In conclusion he asked one thing of his listeners. If they
should ever find one of his sons thinking that to acquire money
and possessions was more important than to seek knowledge, he
asked that they then show his son how he was neglecting what
he needed most, as Socrates himself had shown so many.

"If you do this," he said, "you will be treating both me and my
sons well.

"Now I see that it is time for me to leave. I shall go to my
death, while you go to continued life. But which of us goes to
what is better, is known only to God."

12 / After the trial

Socrates was led away, and his sorrowing friends went home, expecting never to see him again. But on the day before the trial something had happened which, they suddenly recognized, was of inestimable value.

On that day a priest had wreathed the stern of a ship that was to bear to Delos, Apollo's birthplace, the sacred embassy sent by Athens every year to honor the god of light and inspiration. The time between the consecrating of the ship and its return was a holy period, in which no one could be put to death by the state.

The sentence voted by the jury could therefore not be executed until the ship had returned. So, although Socrates was kept in prison, friends were admitted to sit with him every day while he led their thought exactly as he had done wherever they gathered in Athens. They must have been painfully conscious that his death hour was drawing nearer, but as they tried to reason out answers to his questions, they might forget for brief periods how soon they were to lose him. Most frequently among them was his friend Crito, who had been closely associated with him from boyhood. Plato had represented Crito as the one to whom Socrates enjoyed giving an account of the amusing meeting with the brothers Euthydemus and Dionysodorus.

One morning when Socrates awoke in prison while it was still dark, he was surprised to see Crito already sitting near his bed.

"How in the world did the guard happen to let you in at this hour?" he asked.

"He's used to me, Socrates. Besides, I often give him something."

"But why didn't you wake me up at once?"

"You were sleeping so comfortably," Crito replied, "that I couldn't bear to. Indeed I was amazed that even at this dreadful time you should be taking things so easily."

"It would be strange, Crito, if at my age I should resent having to die."

"Other men just as old do resent it."

"I know they do. But tell me why you came so early."

"To bring you sad news—news hard for every one of us to bear, and hardest of all for me."

"That the ship from Delos has arrived?"

"Not yet. But men from Sunium say they saw it there, so it will be here very soon.

"Oh, " he continued urgently, "listen to me, Socrates! There is still time for you to be saved. Simmias has come from Thebes in Boeotia, bringing a large sum for your escape. His friend Cebes will be glad to add to it, and so will many others.

"If you die, I shall lose a friend who can never be replaced. And I hate to think of how people who do not know us well will accuse me of not trying to save you, rich as I am. As if wealth could mean more to me than you!"

"Dear Crito," said Socrates gently, "let us consider this matter with care. The principles I have held highest all my long life, I cannot cast aside because of what people may think. I have always been the kind of man who can be convinced only by logical reasoning. Let us consider now whether I should do right in escaping. If not, then whatever the consequences, I must remain. Stop me at once, if I say anything you can refute. I will listen."

Crito gazed at him sadly as he continued, "We have often maintained that one should never do wrong, not even to persons who have wronged him. This we have asserted, though the majority would not agree with us. Were we mistaken? Or is injustice always evil and disgraceful?"

"It is."

"Think carefully, Crito, whether you really mean what you are saying. This is what we have said, and to me it still seems true. But if you do not agree, admit it and explain your reasons."

"I certainly agree."

Socrates rarely made a long speech, but when he did, he was likely to give it in the form of a dialogue, either real or imagined. This time, to emphasize his point more vividly, he personified the laws of Athens as questioning him. This made the occasion more solemn than if he had been facing a mortal questioner. A human being is susceptible to many influences, but there is a kind of impersonality about laws, established after serious thought and by general agreement, that gives them dignity and weight.

"Imagine," Socrates said, "that I was about to make my escape, when suddenly the laws of the city stood before me and demanded, 'Tell us, Socrates, exactly what you are intending to do. Are you not planning to destroy us, so far as lies in your power? Can a government continue to exist in which legal decisions have no strength, but can be overthrown by any individual at will?' I might answer, 'The government has injured me by imposing a sentence that is wrong.'"

"You could indeed say that," Crito interposed.

"The laws might continue, 'Your parents were married according to us, the laws of Athens, and under us you were well educated. In a sense, you are our child, as your father was before you. You never wished to have been trained elsewhere, for to us you are indebted for a better education than you could have obtained at any other place in the world.

"'When you were sent into battle for us and for your country, you accepted the chance of death. As in battle, so in a court of law you must do what your country orders. There is a regular procedure for changing the laws if they prove to be unjust. This, and not violence, is right. It is also a fact that any Athenian who does not like the laws is always free to go to another Greek state, taking all his property. So he who remains has entered into an implied contract that he will do what we command.

" 'What is more, at the trial you might have proposed the penalty of exile. Then you could have gone elsewhere without disobeying any law, but acting like a free man. Now you are intending to run away like a slave. If you escape now, you will prove yourself a corrupter of law, and therefore likely to corrupt not only young men, but those of every age. You will violate the most sacred laws because of a clinging desire to live just a little longer. If you stay, you will die as a sufferer, not a doer of wrong, a victim not of the laws, but of men. Listen to us, Socrates, not to Crito.'

"These are the words I keep hearing, Crito, and I can think of nothing else. Anything you may say contrary to them will be said in vain. But if you think you will accomplish something, speak."

Sadly Crito said, "No, Socrates. I have nothing to say."

"Then, Crito, let us accept the situation, since this is the way God leads."

Like the days in prison and countless others in the preceding years, the last day of Socrates was passed in philosophic discussion. This time the talk centered on the possibility that a man's soul may survive after death.

The main participants with Socrates were Simmias and Cebes. Simmias was well known among men interested in philosophy for his never-satisfied desire to talk about it, while his friend Cebes was thought to be particularly difficult to convince. Crito was present, as well as his son Critobulus, and the excitable Apollodorus, whose emotions were constantly driving him to extremes. But he had a good memory and could give a complete account of the speeches that had made Agathon's dinner significant.

Other Athenians were present, among them some who had been friends of Socrates for years, like Menexenus, who had introduced the boy Lysis, and Ctesippus, who had admired Cleinias and taken part in the talk with Euthydemus.

A devoted foreigner, Phaedo from Elis, was chosen by Plato to be the narrator of the dialogue bearing his name. The author of this deeply impressive work referred to himself only with the brief statement, "Plato was sick."

Nothing less than actual incapacity, we may be sure, could have kept him away. Whatever the physical manifestation may have been, the cause was surely the violent emotional agony produced by knowledge that his city was about to cut short the life of Socrates—this man whose intellectual and ethical influence had been uplifting the minds of so many Greeks.

The dialogue begins with Phaedo, on his way home from Athens, being asked in Phlius by some philosophers to tell them how Socrates died. They had heard about the trial, and that Socrates was compelled to drink the poisonous hemlock, but they wondered why so much time elapsed before the sentence was executed. When Phaedo explained about the sacred embassy to Delos, they urged him to tell whether any friends were allowed to be with Socrates at the time of his death.

"There is nothing that I enjoy as much," Phaedo replied, "as talking about Socrates—except hearing someone else do so."

"We feel exactly the same way," another philosopher said. "Don't omit even the smallest detail that you remember."

"The strangest thing about it," Phaedo commented, "was that I could hardly believe that he was to die at sunset. He seemed so fearless and his thought so noble that I was not grieving. Yet I could not feel the intense pleasure I usually enjoy whenever the talk is about philosophy. It was the same with the others. Sometimes we surprised one another by bursting into laughter, but the next moment we might feel tears in our eyes, Apollodorus most of all. You know how completely he is carried away by his emotions."

"Indeed we do," they agreed.

The close friends of Socrates had been in the habit of meeting early in the morning at the court where the trial had been held and talking until the doors of the nearby prison were opened. Then they went in and passed the entire day with him. The last morning they met earlier than usual, because on the previous evening when they were leaving, they heard that the ship from Delos had arrived. Now at their knock, the doorkeeper came out and told them to wait.

"The officials are with Socrates," he said. "They are removing his chains and telling him he is to die today."

When his friends were admitted, they found Xanthippe, his wife, sitting beside Socrates, holding their baby boy. She had apparently been with him for some time, but at sight of them she exclaimed, "O Socrates, this is the last time you and your friends will talk together," and began to sob.

Socrates turned to Crito and asked him to see that someone accompanied her home. This has been criticized as heartless, but it is unlikely that such was the impression made on the Athenians who first read it. Xanthippe clearly recognized the need of Socrates to spend his last hours in the same manner in which he had passed all of his days. When friends visited a man in ancient Athens, his wife never remained with them, but went to the rooms reserved for the women of the household. Socrates also was, as always, quick to understand, and he probably knew that she too needed the support of a sympathizing companion, and that Crito would choose the right one of his attending slaves.

Then Socrates sat up on his bed, bent his leg and began to rub it, saying, "How strange it is that pleasure and pain are called opposites, yet whenever one comes to a man, it is likely that the other will follow. I believe that if Aesop had thought of this, he would have added a fable about it to the others he had composed.

The chain had caused a pain in my leg, but now that it is freed, I feel a pleasant relief."

"I'm glad you mentioned Aesop," said Cebes. "That reminded me of a question the poet Evenus asked me the other day. He wanted to know why you, who had never written anything, were putting some of Aesop's fables into verse, and had also composed a hymn in honor of Apollo. Do tell me now. He is sure to ask me again."

"It was because of a thought that came to me lately," said Socrates. "A number of times in my life I have dreamed that I was being told to make music. I had always thought that this referred to the study of philosophy, which is the finest pursuit, and to which I have devoted my life. I was being told, I believed, to do what I had been doing, just as a man who is in a race may hear a bystander shout, 'Run! run!' when he is already running. But in case I might have been mistaken in interpreting the dream this way, I decided to compose some verses. Tell Evenus that I have no intention of rivaling him, for I know I couldn't. But tell him also to follow me as soon as he can, for I am today to go to my death."

"What a message for a man like him!" exclaimed Cebes. "I see him often, Socrates, and from all I have observed, I should say he will never accept this advice."

"Isn't he a philosopher?" Socrates asked.

"I think he is."

"Then he will be willing to die, though he will not take his own life, for that is said not to be right."

"Why is that said? I have heard others make the statement, but they have never been able to make the reason clear."

"What I say will be only an echo of what I have heard," said Socrates, "but I am willing to tell you this. Since I am soon going to leave this life, what better can I do than consider the nature of this change?"

"Then tell me why it should be thought wrong, if death is truly better than life, to kill one's self."

"You mean, I suppose," and Socrates smiled, "why shouldn't a man be his own benefactor, instead of waiting for someone else to do him the service?"

Cebes laughed and said, "Exactly."

"It appears inconsistent, but may not really be so. I believe that the gods are our guardians and wiser than we. Therefore we should wait until they cause our lives to end."

"I think," said Simmias, "that Cebes has you in mind, and feels you are too ready to depart from this care of the gods."

"Do you want me to answer as if I were in court?"

"Yes, I do."

"Then I must try to be more convincing than I was when I spoke before the jury. I am as certain as anyone can be of what he does not actually know, that I shall pass under the care of other gods, equally wise and good. I hope, though I'm not so certain of this, that there is something after death, and as has often been said, something better for men who have been good than for those who were wicked."

"Tell me more of this, so we may share the hope."

"I will try. But I must first hear what Crito is obviously wanting to say."

"Only this," Crito said. "The man who is going to give you the poison has been telling me you should not talk so much now, for talking causes heat that interferes with the poison's action. Sometimes that has made it necessary to compel a man to drink it two or three times."

"Then let him be prepared," Socrates said, "to do this as many times as are needed."

"I was sure you would say that, but he insisted that I tell you."

"And you have done so. Now we can forget about him. I will endeavor to explain to you, Simmias, that the true student of philosophy is trying all his life to approach the state that is completely attained only after death."

"If that is so," said Simmias, "you are indeed right."

"We recognize, don't we, that there is such a thing as death?"

"Of course."

"It is the separation of the thinking part of man from his body?"

"Exactly."

"Does the true philosopher care much about the pleasures of the body? Does he eat and drink chiefly to satisfy the sense of taste, or simply to supply what nature requires?"

"That's all."

"He is seeking primarily to gain knowledge. Is the body with its senses any great help in this? Even sight and hearing, as we often discover, are in some matters inaccurate and mislead us, don't they?"

"Yes, they do."

"Truth is perceived in thought, if at all, isn't it?"

"Yes."

"And doesn't thought work best and accomplish most when least disturbed by anything connected with the body? By sights or sounds or any pain, or even any bodily pleasure?"

"That is true."

"There is another consideration. Is there such a thing as absolute justice—also absolute beauty and absolute good?"

"Certainly."

"Did you ever see any one of these with your eyes, or perceive them with any other bodily sense?"

"Of course not."

"I speak not of them alone, but of absolute greatness and health and strength. Is not the nearest approach to full understanding of their true nature attained by the man who directs his mind alone to consider them in their ultimate purity?"

"That is so," said Simmias.

"I agree," said Cebes, "with the greater part of what you say. But with regard to the soul, men are likely to be incredulous. They fear that when the soul leaves the body at death, it may be nowhere. It may issue from the body like smoke or air and vanish into nothingness. If the soul could hold together, there would be reason to hope that what you have said is true. But both persuasion and argument would be needed to prove that when a man died, his soul still exists and has any power or intelligence."

"True, Cebes. So I suggest that we talk a little about probabilities."

"I should very much like to know your opinion, Socrates."

Most revealing to anyone studying the character of Socrates is the astonishing fact that instead of his friends trying to comfort him just before his death, he spent most of the time in a serious attempt to comfort them.

Each of the two Thebans, Simmias and Cebes, then presented scientific facts that might prove immortality impossible. Phaedo, when giving his account of the last day of Socrates, is represented as saying at this point that these statements produced an unpleasant feeling of uncertainty and confusion in the listeners. It began to seem to them that there were no real grounds for belief in survival.

"But never," Phaedo continued, "have I admired Socrates more than at that moment. His manner toward the young men was gentle and approving, while at the same time he showed that he understood the wounds produced by the arguments and set out to heal them. He might have made one think of a general rallying the army that had begun to flee and urging the men to follow him back into the field of argument.

"At the time," said Phaedo, "I was sitting on a stool close to the much higher couch where he sat. He began playing with my hair, as he sometimes did, saying, 'Tomorrow, Phaedo, perhaps you will cut these curls.' When I assented, he objected. 'Not if you agree with me,' he said. 'That is what you should do today,' he explained, 'if we cannot bring the argument to life again now. We should both then cut off our hair, so that everyone could see that sign of our sorrow. Let us always beware of giving up an argument because we have met unexpected difficulties in proving it. I urge you now to think only of what is true, and not at all of Socrates. If I speak the truth, agree with me. If not, oppose me with all your might. Let me not deceive you and myself with my enthusiasm.' "

A long discussion followed, which concluded with Simmias and Cebes, and the listeners as well, being convinced by Socrates.

It was already late in the day when he said, "Let a man then be of good cheer at death, if during his life he has disregarded the pleasures of the body to seek the pleasures of knowledge, so supplying his soul with the qualities that rightly belong to it— *sophyrosyne* and justice and courage and nobility and truth.

"Soon, I think, I must drink the hemlock. It would be best for me to bathe first, in order that the women may not have the trouble of washing my body after I am dead."

Then Crito asked, "Have you any directions to give us, Socrates? About your children or anything you wish?"

"Do as I have been telling you just now—and not for the first time. If you watch and guide yourselves carefully, you will be doing the best thing for me and my family as well as for your own selves."

"We will do so," said Crito. "In what manner shall we bury you?"

"In whatever way you wish." With a smile he added, "That is, if you catch me and I don't slip away."

Turning to the others, he said, "I've not convinced Crito, my friends, that I am this Socrates who has been talking to you. He thinks I am that other one whom he will soon see lying here dead, and asks how he is to bury me, although I have said so much to show you that when I have swallowed the poison, I will no longer be here, but will have gone away to the joy of those who are blest. The words with which I have comforted you and myself seem to have made no impression on him. So I ask the rest of you now to be a surety for him, as he was surety for me at the trial— except that he assured them that I would remain, while it will be for all of you to assure Crito that I myself have really departed. Tell him not to be depressed when he sees my body being burned or buried. To say the man is being buried himself, my Crito, is not only false, but an insult to the soul. So take courage, dear Crito, and say it is my body you are going to bury, and do this in whatever way you like and consider most in accordance with our customs."

"Then Socrates rose and went into an inner room to bathe. Crito followed, telling us to remain. We waited," Phaedo said, "talking of what had been said that day and the greatness of our sorrow. Each of us felt that he personally was losing one who had been a father to him, and that he thereafter would be an orphan for the rest of his life.

"When Socrates had bathed, his sons were brought to him for a short time. After sending them home, Socrates returned, for the hour of sunset was near. He sat down with us, and very few words were spoken."

The jailer came and said, "Socrates, you are the noblest and gentlest and best man who has ever come here. Even now I know you are not angry with me, as many are. They curse and swear at me, but you understand who are guilty of causing your death. Try to bear this necessity as easily as you can." Bursting into tears, the man rushed to the door.

"I will," Socrates replied, "and may all be well with you. Let someone bring the poison, Crito," he added, "if it is prepared. If not, let them prepare it at once."

"The sun has not yet set," said Crito. "Some men have a good dinner brought to them before they take the poison."

"I know," Socrates replied. "That is because they fancy they are gaining something by that. I am well aware that I should gain nothing. Please do what I ask."

Crito made a sign to one of the attendants, who soon returned with a man bringing the poison in a drinking cup.

Socrates said, "Tell me, my friend, what I should do."

"Only drink it, and then walk around until your legs begin to feel heavy," he replied, handing the cup, "then lie down."

"May I make the usual libation to some god before drinking?" Socrates asked in the easiest and gentlest manner.

"We prepare only just enough."

"I understand," said Socrates, "but I may and do pray to the gods that they bless my journey from this world to the next."

Raising the cup to his lips, he cheerfully drank all it held.

"Up to this point," Phaedo said, "most of us had been able to keep back our tears. But when we saw him drink and watched afterward, in spite of all my efforts, tears poured down my face. I covered my head with my mantle, sorrowing not for him, but for myself because I was being robbed of such a friend. Crito had begun to weep even before me, and Apollodorus had started still earlier, but at this point he broke into a loud cry that shook us all.

"Only Socrates remained calm. 'My strange friends,' he said quietly, 'it was in order to avoid this that I had the women led away earlier, because I have heard that there should be no discordant sound at the time of death. Be strong, and quiet.'

"We were ashamed and forced ourselves to be still."

Socrates walked about until his legs began to feel heavy, then lay down.

After a little, the man who had given the poison pressed his feet and asked if he felt it. He said he did not. Later the man pressed farther up on his legs. They were growing cold and stiff. When this reached the heart he would be gone.

Suddenly Socrates spoke, "Crito, I owe a cock to the god who heals, Asklepios. See that my debt is paid." So he indicated acceptance of death as a cure.

"It shall be done," said Crito with complete understanding. "Is there anything else?"

There was no answer. Crito closed his mouth and eyes.

"So ended the life of our dear friend," said Phaedo. "Of all the men I have ever known, he was by far the best, the wisest, the most just."

These words Plato put into Phaedo's mouth, but they came from his own heart.

The people
around
Socrates

A Brief Guide to Friends, Followers and Foes

Adeimantus *Much older brother of Plato, near the age of Glaucon.*

Agathon *The handsome young poet whose tragedy had won the prize at a festival.*

Alcibiades *A young aristocrat, conspicuous in Athens, who admired Socrates but was not influenced by him.*

Anytus *A popular politician.*

Apollodorus *A highly emotional young follower of Socrates.*

Aristodemus *The admirer who adopted the habit of going barefoot to be like Socrates.*

Aristophanes *The greatest ancient Greek writer of comedy, including* The Clouds.

Callias *A rich Athenian interested in sophists.*

Callicles *A wealthy Athenian in whose house Gorgias stayed.*

Cebes *A friend who came with Simmias from the country north of Athens, hoping to bring about the escape of Socrates from prison.*

Cephalus *The wealthy father of Polemarchus.*

Chaerephon *An ardent young admirer of Socrates.*

Charmides and Cleinias *Each a popular young favorite among Athenians.*

Critias *A friend of Socrates and Gorgias, distinguished as poet and orator. Later he became the most cruel of the Thirty Tyrants.*

Crito *The close lifelong friend of Socrates, about the same age.*

Critobulus *Son of Crito.*

Ctesippus *A friend of Hippothales and admirer of Cleinias.*

Dionysodorus *Brother of Euthydemus.*

Diotima *A priestess who came from Mantinea to Athens, where Socrates declared he had learned much from her.*

Eryximachus *A doctor.*

Euthydemus *With his brother Dionysodorus, he claimed to teach philosophy and politics, but Socrates believed they perverted the objects of both.*

Euthyphro *A respected authority on religious matters.*

Glaucon *The much older brother of Plato, near the age of Adeimantus.*

Gorgias *A celebrated sophist from Sicily.*

Hippias *A sophist from Ceos.*

Hippocrates *An enthusiastic young friend of Socrates.*

Hippothales *A young admirer of Lysis.*

Lysis *A very young boy.*

Lysias *Son of Cephalus and much younger brother of Polemarchus. He became a noted orator.*

Meletus *A young, insignificant poet, who brought the charge against Socrates, at the instigation, many believed, of the politician, Anytus.*

Menexenus *A slightly older friend of Lysis.*

Meno *A Thessalian. Leading a band of mercenaries, he joined the army of Cyrus in Persia in 401 B.C. Xenophon went there in the same year, but with no official rank, at the invitation of his friend, Proxenus, a general. Xenophon disliked Meno and criticized him in the* Anabasis. *Plato's Dialogue bearing his name presents an occasion when Plato may have been present.*

Phaedo *A very young man deeply devoted to Socrates.*

Phaedrus *A young admirer of Socrates, but also of those proficient in trickery with words without any serious thought behind them.*

Plato *An Athenian, born 428 B.C., died 348 B.C. His father's family traced its ancestors back to the early kings of Athens. His mother was the sister of Charmides and niece of Critias. He grew up in a family whose members, through many generations, played an important part in public life.*

Polemarchus *A young friend of Socrates. Later he became a victim of the Thirty Tyrants.*

Polus   *A young admirer of Gorgias.*

Prodicus   *A sophist from Elis.*

Protagoras   *A renowned sophist from Thrace, who visited many cities.*

Simmias   *See Cebes.*

Thrasymachus *A sophist from Chalcedon.*

Xenophon   *An Athenian, born about 444 B.C., died after 357 B.C. He became a successful general, and later a writer. He declared that Socrates, after his death, continued to be missed beyond all others for the help he gave to anyone desiring to attain the highest ethical excellence.*

A key to
the relevant
Dialogues

Bibliography

Kennedy, George. *The Art of Persuasion in Greece*. Princeton University Press, 1963.

Koyre, Alexandre. *Discovering Plato*. Translated by L. C. Rosenfeld. Columbia University Press, 1945.

North, Helen. *Sophrosyne in Greek Literature*. Cornell University Press, 1966.

Dialogues of Plato. Translated with analyses by B. Jowett. Charles Scribner's Sons, 1901.

Plato's Works (Greek text). Edited by John Burnet. Oxford, Clarendon Press. Last reprinted in 1957. (Translations by P.C.W.)

Sinaike, Herman L. *Love, Knowledge and Discourse in Plato*. University of Chicago Press, 1965.

Taylor, A. E. *Plato, the Man and His Work*. The Dial Press, 1936.